DAVE MARTIN

THE FRENCH REVOLUTION

Dedication

'History, a distillation of rumour.' Thomas Carlyle

'Our revolution has made me feel the full force of the axiom that history is fiction and I am convinced that chance and intrigue have produced more heroes than genius and virtue.' Maximilien Robespierre

Acknowledgements

The author and publisher wish to thank Marisa Linton for her advice, expertise and enthusiasm as Academic Consultant and as a contributor on pages 112–113. All judgements, interpretations and errors remain the responsibility of the author.

The Schools History Project

Set up in 1972 to bring new life to history for students aged 13–16, the Schools History Project continues to play an innovatory role in secondary history education. From the start, SHP aimed to show how good history has an important contribution to make to the education of a young person. It does this by creating courses and materials which both respect the importance of up-to-date, well-researched history and provide enjoyable learning experiences for students.

Since 1978 the Project has been based at Trinity and All Saints University College Leeds. It continues to support, inspire and challenge teachers through the annual conference, regional courses and website: http://www.schoolshistoryproject.org.uk. The Project is also closely involved with government bodies and awarding bodies in the planning of courses for Key Stage 3, GCSE and A level.

For teacher support material for this title, visit www.schoolshistoryproject.org.uk.

Although every effort has been made to ensure that website addresses are correct at time of going to press, Hodder Education cannot be held responsible for the content of any website mentioned in this book. It is sometimes possible to find a relocated web page by typing in the address of the home page for a website in the URL window of your browser.

Hachette UK's policy is to use papers that are natural, renewable and recyclable products and made from wood grown in sustainable forests. The logging and manufacturing processes are expected to conform to the environmental regulations of the country of origin.

Orders: please contact Bookpoint Ltd, 130 Milton Park, Abingdon, Oxon OX14 4SB. Telephone: +44 (0)1235 827720. Fax: +44 (0)1235 400454. Lines are open 9.00a.m.–5.00p.m., Monday to Saturday, with a 24-hour message answering service. Visit our website at www.hoddereducation.co.uk.

© Dave Martin 2013

First published in 2013 by
Hodder Education,
an Hachette UK company
338 Euston Road
London NW1 3BH

Impression number   10 9 8 7 6 5 4 3

Year   2017 2016 2015 2014

Typeset in 10pt Usherwood Book
Designed by Lorraine Inglis Design
Artwork by Barking Dog
Printed and bound in Dubai
A catalogue record for this title is available from the British Library

ISBN 978 1 4441 4454 3

Contents

1 The French Revolution: The essentials

△ *The Execution of Louis XVI*, a contemporary engraving. What do you think those organising Louis's execution were worried about?

Abbé
The courtesy title given to all churchmen

It is 21 January 1793. Imagine the scene on a chill and wet winter morning. In the Place de la Revolution a huge crowd, many armed, is gathered around a scaffold. On the scaffold is the **guillotine**. Guarding the scaffold are armed troops and cannon. At 10a.m. a carriage arrives and down from it step two men, Louis XVI, King of France and **Abbé** Henry Edgeworth, the King's chaplain. Edgeworth later described the dramatic scene:

As soon as the King had left the carriage, three guards surrounded him, and would have taken off his clothes, but he repulsed them with haughtiness – he undressed himself, untied his neckcloth, opened his shirt, and arranged it himself. The guards, whom the determined countenance of the King had for a moment disconcerted, seemed to recover their audacity. They surrounded him again, and would have seized his hands. 'What are you attempting?' said the King, drawing back his hands. 'To bind you,' answered the wretches. 'To bind me,' said the King, with an indignant air. 'No! I shall never consent to that: do what you have been ordered, but you shall never bind me...'

The path leading to the scaffold was extremely rough and difficult to pass; the King was obliged to lean on my arm, and from the slowness with which he proceeded, I feared for a moment that his courage might fail; but what was my astonishment, when arrived at the last step, I felt that he suddenly let go my arm, and I saw him cross with a firm foot the breadth of the whole scaffold; silenced, by his look alone, fifteen or twenty drums that were placed opposite to me; and in a voice so loud, that it must have been heard at the Pont Tournant, I heard him pronounce distinctly these memorable words: 'I die innocent of all the crimes laid to my charge; I pardon those who have occasioned my death; and I pray to God that the blood you are going to shed may never be visited on France.'

He was proceeding, when a man on horseback, in the national uniform, and with a ferocious cry, ordered the drums to beat. Many voices were at the same time heard encouraging the executioners. They seemed reanimated themselves, in seizing with violence the most virtuous of kings; they dragged him under the axe of the guillotine, which with one stroke severed his head from his body. All this passed in a moment. The youngest of the guards, who seemed about eighteen, immediately seized the head, and showed it to the people as he walked round the scaffold; he accompanied this monstrous ceremony with the most atrocious and indecent gestures. At first an awful silence prevailed; at length some cries of *'Vive la Republique!'* were heard. By degrees the voices multiplied and in less than ten minutes this cry, a thousand times repeated became the universal shout of the multitude, and every hat was in the air.

So how had things come to such a state, that the King of France, a portly family man who loved nothing better than hunting and making locks should be guillotined by his own subjects who then threw their hats into the air in celebration? And why, in the months after did so many of his subjects follow in his footsteps up those fateful steps to the scaffold where their lives were ended under the blade?

Doctor Guillotin persuaded the Legislative Assembly in March 1792 that all executions should be performed by a humane mechanism. It was first used on 25 April 1792 and became known as the **guillotine**.

Henry Edgeworth

Abbé Edgeworth (1743–1807) was an Irish Catholic priest educated in France. In 1791 he became the confessor of Madame Elisabeth, the King's sister, and she recommended him to Louis when Louis' trial began. Edgeworth accompanied the King on his journey to the scaffold. Immediately after the blade fell Edgeworth melted into the crowd. He remained in hiding in Paris until 1796 then left France and became confessor to the King's brother; the future Louis XVIII. Edgeworth's memoirs were published in 1815.

This activity helps you to consolidate the outline of events. Firstly reduce the story of the French Revolution to seven news headline broadcasts, one for each phase identified in the outline on pages 4–7. These could be one or two sentences long. Then produce a final broadcast lasting up to one minute that summarises the following key themes.

- Who ruled France and how this changed.
- The aims of the revolutionaries and whether they achieved them.
- The scale and pattern of violence.

The story of the French Revolution 1789 to 1804

The execution of the King is perhaps the best known moment of the Revolution but where does it fit into the whole story? It's important at the beginning of your study to gain a good sense of the outline of events. This will give you confidence and a bedrock to build on, adding in more detail (a lot more detail!) as you go.

1788

In 1788 Louis XVI was King of France. He was an absolute monarch which meant that theoretically there were no constitutional limits on his power. One much hated symbol of his power was the *lettre de cachet*. This was a letter, signed by Louis and countersigned by one of his ministers, which allowed the immediate imprisonment of any Frenchman or woman. There was no right of appeal to the courts against this.

The King alone appointed his ministers and could pass whatever laws and follow whatever policies he wished. However, in practice he needed the co-operation of his ministers and of the ruling class.

1789

By 1788 the French government was bankrupt. Louis was forced to call the Estates-General, an elected body that represented all the people of France. When it met in 1789 the complaints that had been building came to a head. The delegates of the common people (known as the Third Estate and including everyone except the nobles and clergy, see page 15) declared themselves to be the National Assembly and swore an oath not to disband until France had a new constitution which gave the people a say in government. This oath was known as the Tennis Court Oath because it was sworn at a meeting in a 'real' tennis court (see page 50)!

To some observers, at this moment a revolution had begun because the delegates of the Third Estate were defying the authority of the King.

By July 1789 there was widespread disorder in Paris after Louis dismissed his popular minister Necker. There were also rumours that the King was planning to use force against the National Assembly. This led to Parisians, helped by the King's own soldiers, storming the **Bastille**, the prison where some of those imprisoned under *lettres de cachet* had been held. If the Tennis Court Oath did not mark the beginning of a revolution then this event certainly did, because Louis had now lost control of Paris.

Bastille
The Bastille was a royal fortress in Paris that was used as a prison. It was seen as a symbol of despotic royal authority

1789–92

Despite the violence this was a moderate revolution so far. Louis XVI still ruled France. The main issue was that the people, represented by the National Assembly, wanted a say in how the King ran the country. Therefore, from 1789 until 1792 France experimented with a constitutional monarchy. This meant that the King's power was now limited (for example, the *lettres de cachet* were abolished) but the key question that everyone found hard to answer was 'How much power will the King have?' This was a tense period, lasting three years, but there were only limited incidents of violence.

Amongst the key moments in this period was the Declaration of the Rights of Man and Citizen in 1789. This was the document of the Revolution, identifying the core values of the revolutionaries – liberty, equality and fraternity.

◁ A contemporary representation of the Declaration of the Rights of Man and Citizen. The images symbolise the idealism and hope of those who created the document. The chains which bound men have been broken and a new age has dawned.

September 1792–June 1793

Towards the end of 1792 the Revolution became more extreme in response to twin threats – the first from internal rebellions against the Revolution and the second from foreign countries at war with France. This had many important results.

- Many people, aristocrats and ordinary people, were imprisoned in Paris because they were seen as opponents of the revolutionary changes. In the September Massacres of 1792 over 1100 of these prisoners were dragged from the prisons and killed without any proper trial.
- An increasingly powerful revolutionary government ordered conscription into the army (the *levée en masse*) to defend the Revolution against France's foreign enemies.
- By the end of the year the King himself had been imprisoned and placed on trial. The verdict was death and Louis was guillotined in January 1793. France was now a republic, ruled by the revolutionaries.

July 1793

Violence increased further. The murder in his bath of the popular revolutionary Marat triggered the Terror, a period in which approximately 240,000 Frenchmen and women died. The Committee of Public Safety became the most important government body in France. It was dominated by Robespierre, who was known as 'The Incorruptible'. He and most of the other members were **Jacobins**, extreme revolutionaries. Characteristic of the many changes they made was a speeding up of the trial process in Revolutionary Tribunals. Anyone charged with *incivisme* (lack of 'civic virtue', or in other words, any form of opposition to the Revolution) could be arrested, tried, convicted and executed within 24 hours. This included ex-aristocrats, ordinary people and even moderate revolutionaries, former allies and friends of those now in power.

Jacobins
This was the name given to members of the Jacobin Club, a political club originally in favour of reform which became more and more revolutionary as time passed

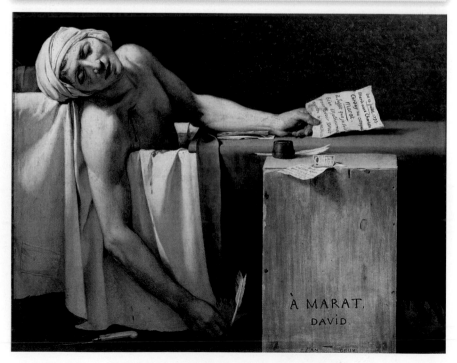

▷ *Marat breathing his last*, painting by Jacques-Louis David. The murder of Marat frightened revolutionaries because it seemed that counter-revolutionaries were fighting back, threatening the Revolution. This made it possible for the more extreme Jacobins to suppress civil liberties in the name of defending the Revolution.

6

◁ The arrest of Robespierre on the night of the 9/10 Thermidor.

As part of their break from the past the revolutionaries introduced a completely new calendar in 1793. One of the new months was called **Thermidor**, the month of heat.

1794–99

The revolutionary government of France had defeated both its internal and foreign enemies yet the Terror continued until July 1794. It ended when a group of revolutionaries, afraid they would be its next victims, plotted to overthrow Robespierre. He was arrested, escaped, rearrested and guillotined in July 1794 in what's known as The Coup of **Thermidor**.

The coup gave its name to the new government, the Thermidorean Government. There was a return to the more moderate policies of the early period of the Revolution and an end to 'government by terror'. However, the leaders did take revenge on the Jacobins and had to prevent attempts by royalists to turn the clock back five years. So violence did continue, but on nothing like the scale of the Terror. The Thermidorean Government was succeeded in 1795 by the more democratic government known as the Directory which controlled France until 1799.

1799

On the 18 Brumaire (November) 1799 the constitutional, and to some degree democratic, government of the Directory was overthrown by Napoleon Bonaparte and the army. Napoleon was a general who had risen through the ranks during the Revolutionary Wars against Britain and other European countries. His victories had made him a national hero. He went on to make himself Emperor in 1804. So France had come almost full circle. Instead of a king it was ruled by an emperor. However, the state he controlled was a more effective modern state with more efficient administration and finances than France before the Revolution.

▽ Napoleon was aged 30 when he took control of France in 1799.

Why is the French Revolution so interesting – and so important?

△ The French Revolution took place over 200 years ago but is far from forgotten. This photograph shows Bastille Day celebrations in Paris on 14 July 2012. It was on that date in 1789 that the people of Paris attacked and captured the Bastille. Bastille Day remains a French national holiday, marked by military parades and ceremonies. What may be more surprising is that Bastille Day is celebrated in other parts of the world, including cities in the USA such as New York and Los Angeles.

As pages 4–7 have shown, the French Revolution was not one brief moment, lasting a week, a month or even a year. The events that made up the Revolution lasted a decade. Think of it as the time it takes for a child of 10 to grow into an adult of 20 and you will gain a sense of the duration of the events of the Revolution.

What was the Revolution? It is obviously about far more than the execution of the King. In fact the Revolution began without any thought of removing the King from power, let alone executing him. The aim of the revolutionaries was, at first, far more moderate – to end absolute monarchy and give many more people a say in government. However, as in the English Civil Wars of the 1640s, the actions and indecisions of individuals, their fears of what might happen and their inability to agree on how the country would be governed as well as counter-revolution and foreign threats, led to escalating violence. As so often in History, events turned out very differently from how anyone had imagined at the start.

This sense of events escalating and changing quickly, explains why these were terrifying, puzzling, exciting, frequently uncertain and anxious times for the people of France. They constantly had to rethink their ideas, decide what kind of government they wanted, what degree of violence they could accept in the name of the Revolution, whether to compromise their principles for the public good or to save their own lives. One of the fascinations of studying the Revolution is discovering how people behaved under such extreme, rapidly-changing conditions. We also have to think about whether the course of events was decided by individuals such as Robespierre or whether such 'great men' were carried along by the wishes of the masses who were at least as interested in having enough to eat as they were in revolutionary ideals.

Another reason for studying the Revolution is that it did not end in the 1790s – the effects of it have continued to reverberate through world events ever since. It had an impact on the revolutionary upheavals in France in 1830, 1848 and 1871, and on revolutions elsewhere, particularly on the Russian Revolution in 1917. The Bolshevik revolutionaries in 1917 saw themselves as the new Jacobins overthrowing the tyranny of another absolute ruler, Tsar Nicholas II. Later still the revolutionary anthem, the Marseillaise, was heard again, sung by Polish nationalists as they fought invading Soviet forces in 1956 and by Chinese protesters in Tiananmen Square in Beijing in 1989. More broadly, the French Revolution gave rise to two major international developments. One was the assertion of universal human rights, the second the emergence of the modern state. In the beginning the revolutionaries wanted to combine the two, to create a constitutional government that would secure and protect personal freedom. But by the 1790s it became apparent that these two ambitions were not necessarily compatible. The increase in state power and centralised government during the Terror came at the expense of individual liberty. Today this same tension can still be seen in societies across Europe and around the world, including our own.

Debates and arguments about the Revolution

The Revolution is so important in the wider pattern of world history that it's not surprising that people have been arguing and debating about it since the day it began. As early as 1790 Edmund Burke wrote his *Reflections on the Revolution in France* in which he said that the revolutionaries were destroying society by attacking religion and the hierarchy of king and aristocracy. Within a year Thomas Paine had written *Rights of Man* declaring that the revolutionaries were advancing individual freedom, human rights and acting as a beacon for all those struggling against repressive governments.

Those arguments between Burke and Paine typify how the Revolution has often been seen as all good or all evil – violence and destruction versus idealism and hope. However, one of the great values of history is learning to question such generalisations and to look for complexity and variety, especially in an event as multi-faceted as the French Revolution. As Professor William Doyle (2001) wrote:

> … few other historical episodes beyond living memory have remained capable of arousing such passionate admiration or loathing. That is because so many of the institutions, habits, attitudes, and reflexes of our own times can still be traced to what we think went wrong, or right, then. Greater knowledge of what occurred will not necessarily change anybody's mind. But it might offer a sounder basis for judgement than the random accumulation of snippets and snapshots which still satisfies most people's curiosity about this crossroads of modern history.

Louis XVI, Marie Antoinette and the Royal family

In the early years of the Revolution the royal family were central figures in events. So, what were Louis and Marie Antoinette like? And how suited were they to dealing with such fast-moving and difficult issues?

Louis

Louis was born in 1754 in Versailles, the son of the **dauphin** Louis-Ferdinand. Following the deaths of his older brother (1761) and father (1765) he became dauphin, heir to the French throne. He was well educated, fluent in English and Italian, and particularly enjoyed hunting and the hobby of lock making.

dauphin
The dauphin was the title given to the heir to the French throne

Some historians have blamed Louis for the failures of his government. They point to him lacking confidence and failing to control the competing noble factions at court. The historian Georges Lefebvre (1939) described Louis as:

> … lacking in will; honest and well-intentioned, he was far from being a great mind …

This negative view was countered by Paul Hanson (2009) who wrote:

> Older descriptions of Louis XVI as intellectually lazy, isolated at Versailles, scarcely engaged with matters of state have given way to more flattering biographies that portray the King as devoted to his subjects, committed to reform, more the victim of circumstance than his own failings.

Somewhere between the two is the assessment of Peter Jones (2010), that Louis:

> … unlike his grandfather, took an intelligent, if fluctuating interest in matters of government.

△ Coronation portrait of Louis XVI from 1774. Louis inherited the throne from his grandfather (Louis XV) in 1774. He was one of an uninterrupted line of Bourbon Kings which stretched back to Henry IV's accession in 1589.

That word 'fluctuating' may well be the key point, suggesting that Louis' involvement in government and willpower to keep pursuing particular policies fluctuated too much to be successful amidst such complex, fast-moving events.

Marie Antoinette

In 1770 Louis married Marie Antoinette, daughter of the Austrian Empress. This was an unpopular marriage as Austria was blamed for France's defeat in the Seven Years' War in 1763. Louis was unable to consummate the marriage for three years. It was not until 1778 that the couple successfully produced a child and 1781 before they produced a male heir.

The problem Marie Antoinette never overcame was her nationality. Austria was the traditional enemy of France and she was often called '*l'Autrichienne*', 'that Austrian woman'. This harmless-sounding nickname is a much deeper insult as '*Autrichienne*' incorporates a pun on the word *chienne*, or bitch.

Hatred of Marie Antoinette's nationality made it easy for people to believe scandal. Her reputation came under attack in the 1780s in a pamphlet called *Le Lever d'Aurore* where an outing to watch the sun rise was twisted into an accusation that she took part in illicit sex and orgies. The author was identified and imprisoned in the Bastille. Nevertheless rumours continued to circulate about Marie Antoinette's sexual conduct, including that she was having affairs with the King's brothers, with women, and that the royal children were bastards.

Historians believe none of these rumours were true but then, as now, mud sticks. As we shall see in later chapters, these rumours undermined confidence in, and support for the monarchy.

△ *Marie Antoinette*, portrait by Elisabeth Vigée-Lebrun (1787). The Queen is depicted as a mother, dressed in simple yet stately clothes, with her children Marie Thérèse, Louis Charles (on her lap), and the Dauphin Louis Joseph. Baby Sophie had died so the Dauphin points to a sad empty cradle.

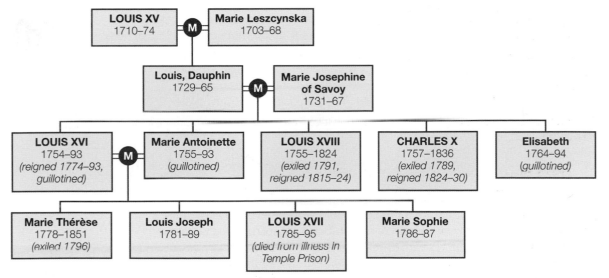

△ A family tree of the French royal family.

A royal revolutionary?

Another member of the royal family who you will meet in later pages was the King's cousin, Philippe, Duc D'Orleans. As a member of the Bourbon royal family he was known as 'a Prince of the Blood'. Married to the richest woman in France he lived a debauched and frivolous life until he became involved in politics in the 1770s and changed his name to Philippe Égalité (which means 'equality') during the Revolution. One view of his role in the Revolution is in the title of Tom Ambrose's 2008 biography *Godfather of the Revolution: The Life of Philippe Égalité, Duc D'Orleans*.

The Ancien Régime (1)

The King and his ministers

The Ancien Régime is the name used nowadays for the French system of government before the Revolution. It was first used in 1790 after the Revolution began – as an insult. It means 'old rule', 'old kingdom' or 'old regime'. The phrase was invented by the Comte de Mirabeau, an early revolutionary, to say that the old system of government and classes was out of date, falling apart, decrepit, over the hill and had to be got rid of, fast!

At the head of the Ancien Régime was the King. In theory Louis XVI was 'an absolute monarch' which means that there were no legal limits to his power over his subjects. At his coronation Louis XVI had sworn an oath to God, not to his subjects. However, in reality his power was based upon the consent of the noble elite and bound by the laws and customs of the kingdom. He therefore did have to take into account other people's views even if the nobles were very few in number.

The King's government consisted of Louis, his advisers and his ministers. This was based in the magnificent Palace of Versailles (shown opposite), roughly twelve miles south-west of Paris. The King did not meet his ministers as a group to make decisions collectively. Instead, Louis met each minister individually to discuss the work of the minister's department. This meant that it was Louis who decided the overall direction of government policy. It also created a situation where ministers worked against each other rather than together and one of Louis' problems was controlling competing **factions** at court. This made it much more difficult to bring in much needed reforms.

Another problem facing Louis and his ministers was the huge variation in laws and customs across France. France had no single representative body, such as the English Parliament, which could pass laws covering the whole country. Since the Middle Ages France's kings had won control of new territories but had allowed these areas to keep local laws and customs unchanged. This meant that Louis XVI's France was a patchwork of different forms of administration, different legal systems, different taxes and different rules on who paid them.

As you can imagine, this bewildering complexity made France difficult to govern. No single solution to a problem could work in every place. Kings had attempted to create one system of royal officials by splitting the country into 36 *généralités* or administrative areas, each under the control of a royal official called an *intendant*. The intendant was responsible for carrying out the policies of the King's government in his region. As representatives of central government, they were often unpopular which led to them being constantly hindered by local law courts and local ***parlements***.

By far the most important of the parlements was the Paris Parlement which had one very significant power – it had to register each royal edict issued by the king before it could become law. Louis could over-ride their objections by using a special royal session known as a *lit de justice* but if he did that too often then confidence in the power of the King's government would weaken and raising money would become increasingly expensive and difficult.

factions
Groups of court nobles competing to secure lands, pensions and well-paid posts such as bishoprics from the King

parlements
These were the major high courts of appeal in France. There were thirteen of them, of which the Parlement of Paris was the most important

△ The Palace of Versailles at the time of Louis XVI.

◁ The Hall of Mirrors at Versailles gives a hint of the opulent lifestyle of Louis XVI, his family and court nobility. Versailles sums up both the grandeur and problems of absolute monarchy. It could create a sense of wonder and pride in France's wealth and power but at times of hardship also emphasised how the King and nobles lived gilded lives, cut off from the people of France.

The Ancien Régime (2)

The Three Estates

French society was divided into three groups, known as the First, Second and Third Estates.

The First Estate – the Clergy

The **clergy** formed less than 0.5 per cent of the population but was powerful and privileged. The Church owned roughly one-tenth of the land making it the largest landowner in France. The political power of the Church was considerable and only Catholics had legal rights. It was only in 1787 that Protestants were given full legal rights such as the right to get married without converting to Catholicism. (Protestants were not given freedom of worship until 1789.) The Church controlled almost all education, most hospitals and **poor relief**. It had extensive powers of censorship and its pulpits were used to publish the King's government's messages.

The clergy also dominated towns, running convents, seminaries, schools, and hospitals as well as churches and cathedrals. In a small town the church could be the largest employer. In the countryside the parish priest or *curé* (often the only educated person in the village) was entitled to receive the tithe, one-tenth of every person's livelihood, to support him. In practice this was not always collected in full but was still a significant tax. However, what the people in the Third Estate disliked far more was that the clergy did not pay taxes. The Church's General Assembly had managed to resist any attempts to take away their tax exemptions. Instead the Church made a voluntary annual grant of about 16 million **livres** to the state – only about five per cent of total church income.

The Second Estate – the nobility

There were roughly **120,000** people who were members of noble families, less than one per cent of the population but together they owned between a quarter and a third of all the land in France. The nobles' greatest privilege was exemption from paying the heaviest tax, the *taille* (a tax on land) and the *corvées royales* (forced labour service to improve roads). They were also exempt from military conscription, although many did volunteer to fight for France by buying commissions as officers in the army and navy. Indeed, all military commissions were purchased which meant, that all the officers were nobles.

There were different levels of nobility:

- The *noblesse de court*, who lived at Versailles, were the most powerful and the wealthiest as only those who could afford it lived at Versailles. They included all the King's ministers, ambassadors, councillors and intendants. Access to the King gave nobles influence over government policy and access to royal patronage of lands, offices and money.

- The *noblesse de robe* lived throughout France, mostly in towns and cities. These were nobles who had purchased legal and administrative offices that carried a hereditary title from the monarch. In 1789 there were over 70,000 of these offices. Buying a **venal office** was a way for the

The **clergy** consisted of 59,500 priests, 60,000 monks and nuns and 5000 non-beneficed people (around 125,000 in total).

poor relief
Payments of food given to the poor

The **livre** was the basic currency of France until 7 April 1795

1 louis = 24 livres

1 livre = 20 sous

1 sou = 12 deniers

Precisely how many nobles there were in 1789 is debatable. The historian Peter Jones suggests **120,000** as an accurate number although some estimates go as high as 400,000.

venal office
An official job or post that could be bought which gave its holder noble status

middle classes to join the nobility but they could also do it through marriage. Men from impoverished noble families married the daughters of rich commoners for their **dowry**. Through both of these methods, gaining noble status was accessible and an estimated 30,000 to 50,000 people became nobles during the eighteenth century.

- The third group of nobles, the great majority, were those who lived on their country estates. Many were no better off than the average **bourgeois**, some were much poorer and were insultingly nicknamed *hobereau* (sparrow hawks) by courtiers. Unsurprisingly these poor nobles were jealous of the court nobles' great wealth and access to royal patronage. Moreover they were very protective of their own status and privileges and determined to enforce the **feudal rights** that their standard of living depended upon. This led them into conflict with their peasants and poorer neighbours.

The Third Estate (the rest!)

The Third Estate consisted of the commoners (anyone who was not a member of the clergy or nobility). This was nearly 28 million people. At the top were the bourgeoisie, mostly living in the towns. These included merchants, industrialists, business people, financiers, landowners, doctors, lawyers and civil servants. As a group they were growing in wealth and numbers, perhaps increasing three-fold between 1660 and 1789. They owned most industrial and all commercial capital, about one-fifth of all private French wealth and roughly one-quarter of all the land. The ambition of most bourgeoisie families was to become noble.

Out in the countryside were the peasants, over 80 per cent of the population. A small minority of richer peasants owned or leased enough land to produce a surplus to sell at market but most farmed at subsistence level and had such a low income that they usually had to work as labourers on other land or as migrant workers in towns. At the very bottom of peasant society were vagrants, perhaps as many as 250,000, who lived in no fixed place. They were feared by the rest of society as outsiders.

The peasantry, the poorest people in society, paid taxes that members of the other Estates did not pay. To the lord of the manor (the *seigneur*) they paid taxes on their grain harvest. Some also paid tax to the lord when their property changed hands. Some worked on the lord's land, while others paid taxes instead of working on the lord's land (work known as labour service). To the state they had to do labour service on the roads (*corvées royales*) and pay the *taille*, the main land tax, and the *gabelle*, a salt tax. They might also be conscripted or have soldiers billeted upon them. Finally they paid the tithe to the Church. As a group their main concern was to stay alive and how hard this was depended very much on the price of bread, the main part of their diet. When prices went up their lives got harder.

dowry
Money or property brought by a bride to her husband on their marriage

bourgeois
Originally meaning 'the citizens of a town', by 1789 the term described the middle classes

Feudal rights dated back to the medieval feudal system and were a variety of taxes paid in money, in kind or through labour by peasants to the landowners. They also included the landowners' control of manorial courts, exclusive rights to hunting and fishing, the right to have a dovecote and the monopoly of operating mills, ovens and wine presses.

2 What were people complaining about in the early 1780s?

△ In this contemporary print an early pioneer of ballooning, Pilâtre de Rozier, is shown at Versailles in 1784. He died the following year in a failed attempt to cross the English Channel.

On 19 September 1783 a new age began, the age of human flight. The Montgolfier brothers demonstrated their new invention, the hot air balloon, at the royal Palace of Versailles. Watching its flight were King Louis XVI and his Queen Marie Antoinette, the *noblesse de court* and a huge crowd of spectators. In a basket attached beneath the balloon were a sheep, a duck and a rooster. Louis was impressed by the flight but not by the stench of the smoke. The Montgolfiers mistakenly believed that it was the smoke that made the balloon rise, not the hot air. Wool, straw and even old shoes were therefore used as fuel to make the densest smoke possible to make the balloon rise. Despite this misunderstanding the balloon (and the sheep, the duck and the rooster) landed safely two miles away after a flight of eight minutes. The flight was a sensation and within a month people were taking to the skies in balloons.

To people watching the balloon flight it must have seemed only right that France was the home of this new age of flight. France appeared to be the most powerful and prosperous nation in Europe. Over the previous century, France's kings had extended its territories by war, diplomacy and inheritance. It held colonies in the Americas, in the Indian Ocean and on the Indian sub-continent. France's population of 29 million people was far greater than its rivals England (with a population of 12 million) and Prussia (with 6 million) and was only perhaps matched by the Austrian Empire (with 20 million people).

Another sign of French vitality was the growth of communications and the spread of new ideas. In 1700 there had been only three newspapers, all published by the government, but the **press** expanded rapidly and by 1785 there were over 80, some published illegally. By 1750, most French towns had a theatre. There was also an expansion of cafés where people would meet and discuss the issues of the day and the growth of salons where people met to discuss art, literature and politics. This was also a period in which popular literature grew too. Adult literacy in France in 1789 was approximately 50 per cent and an increasing number of people were reading books even though they were expensive. As a result of these developments there was more widespread and intense discussion of issues about society amongst the well-educated elite.

At the same time, the common people, the workers in the fields and the towns, also had plenty to talk about at their meeting places – the taverns, the village water-well, at work, at field-gates or in the streets. Their conversations might have been more mundane – the price of bread or taxes, for example, but they were just as important, if not more so, to those who took part. This chapter investigates the range of issues that were causing complaints and discussion in the early 1780s.

Napoleon showed that he understood the power of the **press** when he said, 'Four hostile newspapers are more to be feared than a thousand bayonets.' Modern British politicians have shown that they understood this too!

Salons and Masonic Lodges – meeting places for new ideas

Salons were a feature of Ancien Régime France. An aristocratic hostess would invite men to her home where they would discuss the issues of the day. On occasions political decisions were taken and deals made between the king's ministers in salons. This was one reason why later on in the Revolution when Madam Roland set up her salon, Robespierre was so hostile to it.

Between 1773 and 1779, over 20,000 people joined Masonic lodges, local secret societies with high ideals which set up funds for charities but more importantly were places where men could debate the new ideas about government and society which you will read about later in the chapter from page 24. Duc D'Orleans became Grand Master of the French Masonic order in 1771.

Before going further make sure you have read the insight information on the Ancien Régime on pages 12–15.

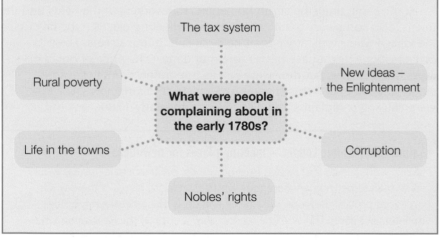
Rural poverty

In 1789 Arthur Young, a British writer on agriculture journeying through France, noted the abject poverty of the rural population. He recorded people with no shoes and ragged, hungry looking children. Another British traveller commented that the French peasants looked more like 'ravenous scarecrows' than human beings. This was not British anti-French prejudice but evidence of real and increasing hardship in the countryside.

Poor harvests were a major reason for increased rural poverty. In the twenty years between 1770 and 1789 there were only three good harvests, which therefore reduced the quantity of food available and inflated prices.

Peasants were also hit hard by the variability of the wine crop which veered between low yields and over supply. Both of these were financially damaging because peasants depended on this crop to supplement their income. In addition the failures of fodder crops (used to feed animals) led to the sale and slaughter of livestock at low prices which further impoverished farmers.

Behind these problems lay even longer-term issues that led to French agriculture being backward in comparison with neighbouring countries. One issue was that many farmers had only small amounts of land (smaller than elsewhere in Europe) and so just concentrated on growing enough to feed their families. Many struggled to do that. This subsistence farming was necessary but meant that peasant farmers did not have the time or could not take the risks of introducing new methods and agricultural improvements such as new crops and new crop rotations to increase crop yields.

The reason for such small estates was the system of land inheritance in which on a man's death his land was divided equally amongst all his heirs rather than going to his eldest son. By 1789 roughly a quarter of French farmland was divided into small plots owned by peasants. Much of the rest was rented out, again in small plots, to peasant share croppers who agreed to provide the labour and tools to work the land and the owner provided the seed and in return received half the crop.

Agricultural problems also affected the woollen industry which was based in the countryside with spinning and weaving done in peasant households to supplement income from farming. The development of mechanisation was only just beginning, so towns like Amiens and Troyes were simply the hubs from which the industry was organised. The woollen industry was affected by the problems in agriculture because peasants were purchasers as well as producers. Poor harvests meant they could not afford to buy woollen goods so the industry declined, reducing the work available to the spinners and weavers. This added to the rural poverty.

■ Add branches to your mind map summarising the aspects of rural poverty that people were likely to be complaining about. The example below suggests some possibilities but is not complete. Make additional notes to record detail so that your map does not get too cluttered.

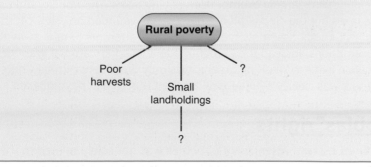

The tax system

▷ The title of this engraving produced in Paris was *Il faut espérer que le jeu finira bientôt* (Let's hope that their game will soon come to an end).

This contemporary engraving sums up the imbalances between the three estates and attacks the inequality of taxation by showing a poor old peasant carrying a bishop and a noble on his back whilst doves eat his seeds. The system of taxation was a major cause of complaint in towns and countryside because, in the eyes of the Third Estate, it was far from fair. The most obvious unfairness was that many of the King's richest subjects, the nobles and clergy, were largely exempt from paying taxes. The nobility did pay some taxes but the clergy did not pay any. As you read on page 14, the Church's General Assembly had resisted royal attempts to take away their tax exemptions. Instead the Church made a voluntary annual grant of about 16 million livres to the King. As this was only 5 per cent of total Church income it was clearly a better deal for the Church than paying taxes!

Nobles' rights

The Third Estate's resentment of nobles was not solely related to their exemption from paying tax. A more direct cause of complaints was the nobles' feudal rights over the peasants on their estates.

Feudal rights dated back to the medieval feudal system. They included a variety of taxes paid by peasants to their lord either in money or in kind (for example, by giving animals instead of money) or by working on the

■ Complete your mind map to record likely complaints about the tax system and Nobles' rights.

lord's lands. Other feudal rights gave lords control of manorial courts, exclusive rights to hunting and fishing (thus denying peasants access to good supplies of food) and the monopoly of operating mills, ovens and wine presses (all of which they could charge people to use).

The nobles also controlled much of the heavy industry – mining and metal working – through investments or direct ownership. Up to 1765 nobles were technically not allowed to trade but in practice many did, making fortunes from sugar plantations in the West Indies, from textiles and from armaments. This monopoly of wealth was one reason why some French people aspired to noble status but many others criticised the nobility's privileged position.

Corruption at court and in the Church

One way in which the French monarchy had raised money was through the system by which over 70,000 offices in the royal bureaucracy could be bought and then became the hereditary property of the purchaser who passed the post on down his family. This 'system' was known as venality. For Louis XVI the advantage was that venality brought in income, around 4 million livres a year, and created a bloc of supporters for the monarchy.

However venality created problems. Not only could it lead to waste through corruption and incompetence but it could block the advancement of those with talent, a major source of resentment in French society. The wealthier bourgeoisie – merchants, industrialists and financiers – did buy these posts but the prices they paid inflated the prices out of reach of the professional bourgeoisie such as lawyers who bitterly resented this.

There were also complaints about the way the Church was run. *Curés* (parish priests) complained they did not receive the entire tithe because it was often collected by abbots and bishops who then paid the *curé* a fixed amount of the tithe yield. As a result *curés* were often quite poor, living on less than 1000 livres per annum while the higher clergy (archbishops, abbots and bishops) enjoyed an income of more than 100,000 livres each year. This made the higher positions very desirable but as they were in the personal gift of the King they were secured by the *noblesse de court* at Versailles for their younger sons. In 1789 all but one of the 135 bishops was of noble birth and a quarter came from just thirteen families. Other problems associated with the nobility's control of the highest positions in the Church were that some bishops were more interested in pursuing political power and so did not live in their dioceses (absenteeism) and some held more than one diocese (pluralism) and rarely visited them.

These issues led to opposition from groups inside the Church. The Jansenists were Catholics who believed that the Pope and the bishops had too much power and were corrupt and venal. However, their criticisms led to the Jansenists coming under increasing persecution by the Church with the Archbishop of Paris in the 1750s denying them the **sacraments**. The persecution of the Jansenists was supported by the monarchy. In response the Jansenists, many of them members of the Parlement of Paris, criticised the Church hierarchy and became involved in opposition to the monarchy itself. Just as they thought the Church should be more conciliar rather than ruled from above by bishops and archbishops, they argued that people should have more power in the nation rather than being ruled by a monarch.

> ■ Complete your mind map to record likely complaints about corruption.

sacraments
Religious ceremonies such as baptism and holy communion

21

Life in the towns

One significant development in eighteenth-century France was the growth of towns. In places this was the result of growth in industries such as silk in Nîmes and Lyons. Foreign trade was another cause with Atlantic ports such as Bordeaux and Nantes trading profitably in coffee, cotton, sugar and slaves with French colonies in the West Indies. Marseille traded profitably with the eastern Mediterranean area. The scale of growth was dramatic. Paris grew by roughly 20 per cent but Lyons and Marseilles by more than 50 per cent and Bordeaux and Nantes by more than 100 per cent. While most French towns were still small, with less than 10,000 inhabitants, rapid growth created serious problems and tensions in the urban populations.

Pays d'états

These were provinces which had held onto a representative assembly of the three orders, whose main role was to negotiate the raising and collecting of taxes with the royal government

Legend:
- ▢ Pays d'états
- –·– International boundaries
- ▤ Boundaries between Généralités
- —— Internal boundaries of central customs area
- ● Place where a Parlement met
- ○ Towns with over 20,000 people
- · Smaller towns

△ Pre-revolutionary France.

Towns were an astonishing mix of rich and poor (but mostly poor) where tensions and anger could be stirred and spread rapidly. Most of France's wealthiest and best educated people lived in towns, the nobles and bourgeoisie, a few manufacturers and the skilled craftsmen who were organised into guilds. Besides these there were the small property owners, shop keepers and artisans. However, the majority of the populations of towns were poor. There was a whole host of unskilled workers (such as 40–50,000 domestic servants in Paris alone, for example) living in over-crowded and unhealthy tenements several storeys high. The **standard of living** in the poorest areas was low with poor water supplies and sewerage systems. These in turn led to the spread of disease and to high rates of infant mortality and low life expectancy. In the 1780s, life expectancy at birth for France as a whole was just 28.5 years.

As with peasants, the main concern of most of the people in towns was having enough to eat. They relied heavily upon bread which typically made up three-quarters of their diet. Therefore sudden rises in the price of grain or bread (which occurred frequently and dramatically) were the triggers for unrest and public disorder, especially in towns where so many people were gathered. Even disorder by peasants tended to happen in towns on market day. There was a belief in French society that the price of bread should be kept low enough for ordinary people to be able to afford it. When prices rose people took direct action, such as threatening bakers and grain dealers, breaking into shops and warehouses and selling bread and grain off at what they thought was a fair price or intimidating local magistrates into fixing prices at a reasonable level.

> Despite extensive poverty and poor **standards of living**, reforming living and working conditions was not noticeably high up on the revolutionaries' agenda in the 1790s once revolution had broken out.

> ■ Complete your mind map to record likely complaints about life in towns.

△ *The Port au Blé and the Port Notre-Dame*, painted by Louis Nicolas de Lespinasse in 1782. Twelve miles north east of the luxuries of Versailles, was Paris, the rapidly-growing capital city of France with a population of roughly 650,000 people.

New ideas – the Enlightenment

This section is about new ideas that led to criticisms of the Ancien Régime, including the power of the Church and absolute monarchy. These ideas were part of an intellectual movement known as the Enlightenment (*c.*1740–*c.*1789) which spread across Europe but had a particularly strong influence in France.

In the mid-eighteenth century, scientific ideas and the practical application of science in technology and industry were making huge advances. Writers and thinkers, using rational thought and logic to analyse society and the world around them, were challenging traditional beliefs and explanations of the world. They pondered ideas about the nature of society and man's relationships with each other, exploring notions of freedom, liberty and equality. This did not go down too well with the absolute monarchies which controlled Europe.

The writers and thinkers who led Enlightenment thinking in France were known as the *philosophes*. They were recognised as a distinct movement from the 1740s onwards. Many of the *philosophes* contributed to the most important work of the French Enlightenment – *The Encyclopaedia* – edited by Denis Diderot, published in 35 volumes between 1750 and 1772. It was a collaborative venture with over 140 contributors, incorporating the main ideas of the French Enlightenment, with the stated aim 'to change the way people think'.

Jean Jacques Rousseau (1712–78)

Rousseau was born in Switzerland but lived much of his life in France. He wrote music, political philosophy and literature and his ideas had a great influence in France both before and during the Revolution. In *The Social Contract* (1762) he developed the idea of the 'general will', that it was the people who were France and not the King. Some historians have argued that this book was not widely read before 1789 and that Rousseau was therefore not that influential. Others have countered that argument by pointing out how similar ideas can be found within his best-selling novels such as *La Nouvelle Héloise* (1761) with its ideas of rural happiness and *Emile* (1762) with its ideas on educating men and women for citizenship. Certainly the government feared his books. They were banned and even publicly burned, prompting Rousseau to say, 'Burning is not an answer'.

Amongst the future revolutionaries who acknowledged that they were heavily influenced by Rousseau's ideas were Madam Roland, Marat and most important of all Robespierre. But it was not just revolutionaries that Rousseau influenced. His idea of the virtues of a simple rural life convinced Louis XVI's father to provide the education of a locksmith for his son, which explains Louis XVI's unlikely hobby of lock making. The same ideas prompted Marie Antoinette to recreate a village at Versailles where she and her courtiers could sample a simple rustic life. The notion of a Queen playing at being a peasant, whilst real peasants starved, later proved to be a public relations disaster for the monarchy.

▷ This table shows the places – Masonic lodges and theatres – and the ways – the *Encyclopédie* and bookshops – in which Enlightenment ideas were spread in French towns and cities. Figures for Paris are very difficult to find, hence the lack of accurate information. (From *The Longman Companion to the French Revolution* by Colin Jones, Pearson Education Limited © Longman Group UK Limited 1988.)

	Population in 1789	Number of Masonic lodges	Theatre: date established	Number of bookshops	Subscriptions to the *Encylopédie*
PARIS	524,186	?	?	?	575
Aix	24,492	13	x (1757)	2	6
Amiens	43,492	4	x (1778)	3	59
Angers	27,596	6	x (unknown)	3	109
Arles	24,700	1		1	nil
Avignon	24,238	8			55
Arras	20,410	5		3	?
Bayonne	20,000	10	x (1777)	2	?
Besançon	20,228	6	x (1775)	12	338
Bordeaux	82,602	22	x (1735)	12	356
Brest	33,852	10	x (unknown)	1	20
Caen	31,902	10	x (unknown)	1	20
Clermont	13,590	7		2	13
Dijon	21,298	4	x (1787)	7	152
Dunkirk	28,548	9	x (unknown)	4	?
Grenoble	24,830	6	x (1765)	1	80
Lille	70,000	7		7	28
Limoges	32,856	4	x (1786)	2	3
Lyons	138,684	33	x (unknown)	30	1079
Le Mans	21,866	4		5	?
Marseille	76,222	17	x (unknown)	10	228
Metz	46,332	17	x (1738)	10	22
Montauban	23,920	7	x (1773)	2	105
Montpellier	33,202	19	x (1752)	7	169
Nancy	33,432	7	x (1707)	17	121
Nantes	64,994	14	x (1749)	6	38
Nîmes	48,360	11	x (1739)	5	212
Orléans	35,594	5		17	52
Reims	30,602	4	x (1773)	8	24
Rennes	20,000	4		6	218
Rouen	64,722	15	x (1774)	30	125
Strasbourg	41,922	15	x (unknown)	7	16
Toulon	30,160	9	x (1765)	2	22
Toulouse	55,068	17		15	451
Tours	31,772	9		5	65
Troyes	30,706	2		3	53
Versailles	44,200	18		6	5

empirical

An empirical approach is based upon observation and experiment and experience

■ Complete your mind map to record the ideas of the Enlightenment that prompted criticisms of the Ancien Régime.

'Do Books Cause Revolutions?'

The historian Robert Darnton (1995) posed this question. Do you think it is possible to argue that books caused the French Revolution just as modern media commentators have argued that Twitter and Facebook/social media caused the Egyptian revolution in 2011? Note: adult literacy in France in 1789 was approximately 50 per cent; adult literacy in Egypt in 2008 was approximately 66 per cent (source Unesco).

Its approach was **empirical**, sceptical and practical. It aimed to give people access to human knowledge and break the power of superstition. Articles dealt with topics like 'reason' but also with agricultural techniques, printing and metalworking. Its scientific approach directly challenged ideas held by the Church and other institutions and caused huge controversy. Some elements in the Church wanted it to be suppressed.

The most influential *philosophes* were Montesquieu, Voltaire and Rousseau. In their writings they expressed a profound dislike of organised religion and discussed how social and political institutions might be changed for the good of the people. This brought into question the institutions and values of the Ancien Régime but, whilst the *philosophes* were certainly critics of the regime, they did not advocate revolution. Montesquieu criticised royal absolutism and despotism but argued that it was the role of the aristocracy to limit royal power rather than ordinary people. He was a member of a *parlement* for many years. Voltaire criticised the Catholic Church and religious intolerance but still believed that religion was necessary to preserve public morals amongst the masses and later defended royal authority. Both of these writers praised the British parliamentary system. Perhaps only Rousseau went further: he suggested that a despotic monarch could be overthrown by their subjects and advanced the idea that sovereignty resided in the people rather than in the person of the king. In the *Social Contract*, he talked of the benefits of a collective 'general will'.

As this was a period in which popular literature grew too the *philosophes* achieved a wider audience for their ideas through fiction. They considered that stories and plays provided an excellent vehicle for making their ideas about society accessible. Voltaire's acclaimed novel, *Candide*, was banned for blasphemy and its mockery of religion. Voltaire, who was probably France's greatest *philosophe*, ended up in the Bastille!

America was another source of ideas challenging the Ancien Régime. In 1778 Louis XVI had taken the fateful decision to enter the American War of Independence, fighting against Britain. The American colonies had been in revolt against Britain for over two years and many in France were sympathetic to the American colonists' pursuit of freedom (liberty) and democracy. Some idealistic French aristocrats, notably the Marquis de Lafayette, had already crossed the Atlantic to enlist in the American forces. Britain was defeated and the colonies got their independence.

When Lafayette and the 8000 troops who had served in America returned home after 1783 they brought with them the renewed ideas of liberty and democracy and the example and experience of how an existing political authority could be overthrown and a new order built in its place.

Summary: What were people complaining about in the early 1780s?

There were clearly plenty of reasons why many people were unhappy and even angry with the nature of French society by the early 1780s. In addition, the Enlightenment was spreading new ideals which were filling some people's minds with possibilities for future reform. However, it would be a mistake to assume that complaints and even anger necessarily led to revolution. Many of these problems had existed for many decades and had not led to revolution in the past. For example, there had been considerable criticism of Louis XVIs' predecessor, his grandfather, Louis XV, and of the extravagance and corruption at Versailles but no attempt had been made to overturn the power of the monarchy.

We can, with hindsight, see that the rapidly growing towns were the places where public opinion could exert its greatest influence because there were so many people gathered together in one place and news and rumour spread rapidly. Therefore it would be the towns where risings of workers, affected by the costs of food, could have a major impact. However, that is with hindsight. We need to remember that the *philosophes* debating in their salons and the commoners grumbling in the taverns were totally unaware of what lay ahead. It was a huge and unforeseeable step from complaints to revolution.

■ Concluding your enquiry

1 Review your completed mind map by comparing your version with those of others in your group and discussing possible amendments and additions.

2 Use different colours to identify the issues that you think were:

   a) of most concern to the Third Estate

   b) most likely to lead to disorder and violence

   c) most likely to lead to change in the way France was governed.

3 Use the mind map to create a possible agenda for reform, identifying priorities for the King's government. In addition, note those things which the King could do nothing about.

Marquis de Lafayette (1757–1834)

Lafayette was a wealthy aristocrat who became a hero of the American Revolution. On his return to France he was one of those liberal aristocrats in favour of reform, a member of the Masons and a founder of the Society of the Friends of Blacks. In the Assembly of Notables he supported the calling of the Estates-General.

He was elected as a Second Estate deputy and enjoyed great popularity with the Parisian crowds, being elected the first commander of the new National Guard. His actions saved the Queen during the dramas of the October Days of 1789 but Marie Antoinette hated him for his support for reform, and the royal family regarded him more as their gaoler than as a supporter. Increasingly worried by the direction the Revolution was taking, he tried to work for constitutional monarchy. After the royal family's attempted escape to Varennes in 1791 he was blamed by the Jacobins and after ordering the shooting of unarmed demonstrators at the Champs de Mars he was completely discredited.

He commanded an army in the Revolutionary War but in 1792, horrified by events, he first tried to use his army against the Jacobins and then when that failed defected to the Austrians. He was imprisoned by the allies and, after an unsuccessful escape attempt, held in solitary confinement until 1795 when his wife managed to reach him and share his captivity. Released in 1797 he was eventually allowed to return to live on his estates in France under Napoleon.

3 Why did Louis XVI call the Estates-General?

In August 1788 a meeting of the Estates-General was called for the following February. The Estates-General was an elected body that contained representatives (called deputies) of each of the three estates of French society, the Clergy, the Nobility and the Third Estate. This was a remarkable event because it was only called to meet in times of national crisis and the last time it had met had been 175 years earlier, in 1614.

The importance of the calling and meeting of the Estates-General cannot be underestimated in the story of the French Revolution. Once it met it provided a forum for individuals to voice the ideas, complaints, prejudices and aspirations that had been building in France for years. What happened there triggered the early events of the Revolution. So why did Louis do it? Why did he call the Estates-General?

Princes of the Blood

The King's seven closest male relatives

Certainly some of his closest advisers, the **Princes of the Blood,** warned him that radical ideas would spread once the Estates-General met. They wrote to Louis on 12 December 1788:

> Sire, the State is in danger; your person is respected, the virtues of the monarch ensure the homage of the nation; but Sire, a revolution is brewing in the principles of government; it is being brought on by the ferment of opinion. Reputedly sacred institutions, which this monarchy has made to prosper for so many centuries, have become matters for debate, or are even described as injustices.

Clearly they were alarmed at the spread of ideas and the debates taking place, though it's a sign of the divisions at all levels of French society that two of the seven princes did not sign this letter. The King's younger brother, the Comte de Provence, and his cousin the Duc D'Orleans, were both in favour of some reform.

Chronology of events

1776	Jacques Necker joined the government to try to solve economic problems
1778	France joined the American War of Independence, increasing her economic problems
1781	Necker resigned from the government
1783	American War of Independence ended
	Calonne became Finance Minister, again aiming to solve the now greater economic crisis
1787	Assembly of Notables called by Louis to agree to new taxation. They refused
1788	Calonne dismissed and replaced by Brienne with no more success
	Louis summoned Estates-General to meet in 1789 after elections.

Enquiry Focus: Why did Louis XVI call the Estates-General?

This flow diagram shows the sequence of events that led up to Louis' momentous decision to call the Estates-General. The questions on the diagram will guide you through the events described in this chapter. The best way to tackle this is to read the whole chapter through once without stopping to take notes or answer any questions. This will give you an overview of the issues. Then read it again slowly, making notes to answer the questions in the diagram.

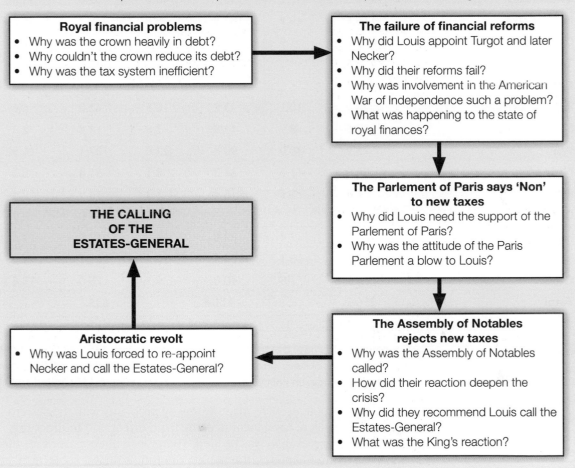

Royal financial problems
- Why was the crown heavily in debt?
- Why couldn't the crown reduce its debt?
- Why was the tax system inefficient?

The failure of financial reforms
- Why did Louis appoint Turgot and later Necker?
- Why did their reforms fail?
- Why was involvement in the American War of Independence such a problem?
- What was happening to the state of royal finances?

The Parlement of Paris says 'Non' to new taxes
- Why did Louis need the support of the Parlement of Paris?
- Why was the attitude of the Paris Parlement a blow to Louis?

THE CALLING OF THE ESTATES-GENERAL

The Assembly of Notables rejects new taxes
- Why was the Assembly of Notables called?
- How did their reaction deepen the crisis?
- Why did they recommend Louis call the Estates-General?
- What was the King's reaction?

Aristocratic revolt
- Why was Louis forced to re-appoint Necker and call the Estates-General?

Royal financial problems

When Louis XVI inherited the throne in 1774 his most pressing problem was money. The monarchy was heavily in debt largely due to the costs of fighting foreign wars. The War of Austrian Succession (1740–48) and the Seven Years' War (1756–63) had cost an estimated 2.8 billion livres.

Louis could not pay off the royal debts. As the table on page 30 shows, even in peacetime royal income was not enough to cover expenditure. The key reason for this was the cost of the interest on the debt. To make up the shortfall, the crown borrowed from international banks and financiers but this made the problem worse in the longer term. And the fact that France did not have a central bank to manage the process made raising loans more difficult and more costly.

	1751		1775		1788	
Income	in livres	as a %	in livres	as a %	in livres	as a %
Royal domain	5.6	2.2	9.4	2.5	51.2	10.8
Clergy	14.3	5.5	3.0	0.8		
*Dons gratuits (pays d'état, etc)**	8.0	3.1	23.9	6.3	20.6	4.4
Direct taxes	109.0	42.2	150.7	40.0	163.0	34.6
Indirect taxes	116.6	45.1	183.9	48.8	219.3	46.5
Other	5.0	1.9	6.3	1.6	17.5	3.7
Total	258.5		377.2		471.6	
Expenditure						
Royal Household	26.0	10.1	43.0	10.5	42.0	6.6
Foreign affairs	22.8	8.9	11.8	2.9	14.4	2.3
War	76.9	30.0	90.6	22.0	107.1	16.9
Navy	28.8	11.2	33.2	8.1	51.8	8.2
Public works	6.4	2.5	5.4	1.3	14.9	2.4
Charity					19.0	3.0
Pensions, etc	18.9	7.4	33.0	8.0	47.8	7.6
Servicing the debt interest	71.8	28.1	154.4	37.5	261.1	41.2
Other	4.7	1.8	40.0	9.7	75.0	11.8
Total	256.3		411.4		633.1	

*This means the amount of tax the pays d'états (see page 22) had individually negotiated with the royal government.

△ Government income and expenditure in three peace years, 1751, 1775 and 1788, figures in millions of livres. (From *The Longman Companion to the French Revolution* by Colin Jones, Pearson Education Limited © Longman Group UK Limited 1988.)

direct tax
Tax paid on the income or profits of the person who pays it

indirect tax
Tax paid on goods or services purchased

Farmers-General
These were a significant feature of society – they were the largest employer in France after the King's army and navy

■ Answer the questions in the flow diagram on page 29 for the section on 'Royal financial problems'.

Louis' financial problems were made worse by problems with the system of taxation. The bulk of royal income came from **direct** and **indirect tax** which delivered far less than was needed. There were three reasons for this.

1. As discussed in Chapter 2, the nobles, the King's richest subjects, were exempt from most taxes. While they did pay a small amount of tax they contributed very little to solving the King's financial problems.

2. Tax collection was both chaotic and incomplete because of all the regional differences. Brittany and the salt tax (*gabelle*) provide a good case study. Brittany's inhabitants were exempt from the tax. Their neighbours in Anjou, Maine, Normandy and Poitou were not. This led to widespread cross border salt smuggling, so much less tax was collected despite the government employing roughly 23,000 people to stop it.

3. The system of 'tax farming' reduced the crown's income. Every six years the crown made a contract with a syndicate called the **Farmers-General**. They paid an agreed sum to the crown in advance, for the right to collect taxes such as the *taille*. The difference between what they paid to the crown and what they collected was their profit. Even taking into account the costs of collecting taxes the monarchy might still have received a greater tax income if it had collected taxes itself.

The failure of financial reforms

In the early years of his reign (which began in 1774) Louis tried to tackle the problem of the royal finances through reforms. In 1776 he appointed Turgot as Controller General, the minister responsible for royal finances. Turgot was influenced by the ideas of the physiocrats, economists who believed that free trade was the key to increasing government income because free trade would lead to economic growth and this growth would mean that more taxes would be paid to the government. Free trade meant that all state regulations, tolls and price controls should be ended. Turgot therefore tried to increase trade by removing price controls and abolishing guilds. He also tried to reform taxation by proposing a property tax intended to increase direct tax revenue. Both Turgot's reforms and the way he went about them aroused great hostility from those whose interests were threatened and Louis dismissed him.

Turgot's replacement in 1776 was Jacques Necker, a Swiss banker with a brilliant reputation. Necker tried a different route of reducing royal expenditure and increasing the royal share of farmed taxes. One of his targets for cuts was venal offices. Two examples show the extent of the problem and why it was so hard to reform.

■ The first example is the 48 posts of Receivers-General who collected direct taxes. Necker abolished these posts and replaced them with just 12 officials who were answerable to his department. Needless to say all of those who held these 48 posts, and the many staff they in turn employed, were not happy.

■ The second example was in the royal household at Versailles where over 400 ceremonial offices in the King's kitchen were abolished. Once again the court nobles who held these offices were unhappy.

So in both examples above and in others, Necker was offending the vested interests of property owners and those who held venal offices, and he also incurred the hostility of Marie Antoinette, both for exposing royal finances to public attention and also for harming the interests of her clique (see page 33).

Necker also had to deal with the impact on royal finances of the American War of Independence (1775–83). In 1778 Louis XVI took the fateful decision of entering the war against Britain. The American colonies had been in revolt against Britain for over two years and many in France were sympathetic to the American colonists' pursuit of freedom (liberty) and democracy. More importantly this was France's chance to reverse the defeat they had suffered at Britain's hands in the Seven Years' War (1756–63) when France had lost control of its colonies in Canada, India and several West Indian islands. Now it had an opportunity to defeat and humiliate the British, which it did. Britain lost the war and the former British colonies became the United States of America. However, despite winning the war militarily in some ways France also lost. The war was hugely expensive and cost possibly as much as 1.3 billion livres. Therefore the financial problems of the monarchy, which Louis and his ministers had so far failed to solve, were now made much worse.

Not all of Louis' minsters had been in favour of war. When he first came to office and examined the royal finances Turgot had warned, 'the first gunshot will drive the State to bankruptcy'. His successor, Necker, instead claimed that the royal finances were in good order and that the war could be funded by loans and that is what he proceeded to do. This bad advice and Louis listening to it, meant that the royal debt continued to rise. The historian, Simon Schama, describes Necker's claims 'as exactly the kind of spurious good cheer that led the French monarchy down the primrose path to perdition'.

Despite these increasing problems, in 1781 Necker issued the first public report on royal finances to show that, in his view, they were in good order. However, some of the minor details of court expenditure were seized upon by the enemies of the monarchy as examples of extravagant royal spending. This lost Necker more friends and later that year he resigned. His successors reversed his reforms. And so the financial problems continued unresolved because of hostility to all reforms. The crown survived by borrowing but all the time the King's debts increased.

■ Answer the questions in the flow diagram on page 29 for the section on 'The failure of financial reforms'.

The Parlement of Paris says 'Non' to new taxes

From 1783 Louis' chief minister, the Vicomte de Calonne, managed the royal finances by selling offices and by lavish spending. Whilst this may seem a paradox (because it did exactly what previous ministers had been trying to stop), the lavish spending maintained confidence in the monarchy which meant that it could raise loans. However, Calonne and others recognised that this could not continue indefinitely and that reform was still very much needed. He hoped that there would be an opportunity for reform in 1787 when a number of taxes were due for renewal. But events overtook him. Calonne was unsuccessful in raising loans in 1785 and early 1786 and so in August 1786 he told Louis XVI than the government was on the verge of bankruptcy. The failure to raise loans and the high interest costs of the royal debt meant that new taxes were urgently needed.

Whilst Louis was notionally an absolute monarch (see page 4), in order to raise new taxes he needed the agreement of the judges of the Paris Parlement. The Paris Parlement was a legal court but with additional powers. The key one was that a royal edict did not become law until it had been registered by the Parlement. Louis could over ride their objections with a special royal session, a *lit de justice*, but such opposition would knock public confidence in the monarchy and make royal borrowing even more expensive. Not only that, the judges of the Paris Parlement had a history of resisting royal power and they had done so in 1785 when they refused to agree to new loans. Relations between Louis' ministers and the Parlement were strained. Essentially the Parlement had no confidence in Calonne. Calonne feared that it would reject his reforms and say no to new taxes so he changed tactics.

■ Answer the questions in the flow diagram on page 29 for the section on 'The Parlement of Paris says 'Non' to new taxes'.

The Assembly of Notables rejects new taxes

Calonne's advice was for Louis to call an Assembly of Notables, 144 men selected by the King. Louis did. The notables included leading members of the *parlements*, the seven Princes of the Blood, important nobles and churchmen. They were expected to agree with Louis. They met in February 1787 to consider a number of proposals that might resolve the financial problems. The key proposals were a new land tax payable by all landowners with no exemptions and the creation of regional assemblies to implement new taxes. However, the Assembly of Notables did not agree. They might have been in favour of some reforms, including that all should pay taxes, but they argued that the approval of the French nation was required and that Louis should call the Estates-General.

◁ In this contemporary caricature of the Assembly of Notables, Calonne is depicted as a monkey asking the assembled birds what sauce they would like to be eaten with. Note his knife. The notice reads 'Buffet de La Cour, Calonne Cuisiner' which translates as 'Meal of the Courtyard, Calonne cook'. The caption to the cartoon read: 'My dear governed ones, I have called you to know with what sauce you would like to be eaten.' They reply: 'But we don't want to be eaten at all.'

There are differing explanations from historians about why the Notables did this, largely because of the variety of views amongst the Notables themselves. The first explanation, that the Notables were simply selfishly protecting their own interests by resisting paying taxes, was true for some, although others felt the proposals did not go far enough. The second explanation is that they were making a principled stand against royal despotism following the same line of argument as the Paris Parlement. This too was true for many Notables as was the third reason: that they blamed Calonne's overspending for the problem. The fourth explanation was that it was the result of Marie Antoinette and her **Polignac clique** at court plotting against Calonne as part of the constant competition for offices and patronage. Thomas Kaiser (2000) made the case when he wrote:

The Duchess de Polignac was a close friend of Marie Antoinette and used her influence to promote the interests of her family and friends. Together they were known as the **Polignac clique**.

■ Answer the questions in the flow diagram on page 29 for the section on 'The Assembly of Notables rejects new taxes'.

… the queen partly filled the political void around Louis, who had seen his best hopes smashed by the Assembly of Notables' rejection of Calonne's reform programme. Soon thereafter she successfully installed her candidate, the archbishop Lomenie de Brienne, as principal minister, …

Brienne's appointment after Calonne's dismissal was viewed as a sign of the Queen's increasing power and a means of expanding it, as was the re-appointment and dismissal of Jacques Necker later on. No wonder that she was blamed during this period for having engineered the state's fiscal crisis and acquired the title of 'Madame Deficit'.

The attitudes of the nobles – variety not uniformity

It is all too easy to ascribe one set of views to a particular group like the nobles. We might suspect that they all wanted to protect their 'vested interests' and privilege and so would not want anything to change. However, real life is always more complex and the nobles took a variety of positions. Some did just want to protect what they had. Others were concerned about the absolutist system of government and wanted more power delegated to other groups because they could see the system was not working well. Some of the nobles in the *parlements* wanted to see reform. But there were other nobles who were quite progressive, some influenced by the ideas of the philosophes, who thought that the institutions of France needed to change to bring France into the modern world. Most of these would probably have wanted the King to stay but with his power curtailed and a more representative government. For an example of a really radical noble, see Philippe Égalité on page 125.

Aristocratic revolt

The refusal of the Notables to approve the new taxes meant that Calonne had failed. Louis replaced him with Lomenie de Brienne. Brienne brought forward proposals for reform, still including the land tax. Once again the Assembly of Notables refused to support this and so they were dissolved. Instead the new reforms were presented to the Paris Parlement to be registered. When the Parlement also refused Louis exiled them to Troyes and used a *lit de justice* to force the registration of the reforms. This provoked an aristocratic revolt. Nobles and clergy met to discuss how to defend the powers of the *parlements*. If proof was needed that Louis was not an absolute monarch then this was it.

At that point lack of money proved decisive. In August 1788 the royal treasury had to suspend all payments – the crown was bankrupt. Now Louis was forced by the nobles and by popular opinion to reappoint Necker as chief minister. Necker was seen as the only man who could restore the royal finances. He was also an advocate of reform. Most importantly Louis had run out of options. The Assembly of Notables would not support his tax reforms, neither would the Parlement of Paris. He could not raise money through loans so he had no choice but to agree to call the Estates-General for May 1789 even though he had been warned of its dangers by the Princes of the Blood.

■ Answer the question in the flow diagram on page 29 for the section on 'Aristocratic revolt'.

Summary – Why did Louis XVI call the Estates-General?

The calling of the Estates-General was an admission of failure, a failure of royal government to address the problem of the national debt and government finances. Just as a recent US President attempting to get elected famously said, 'It's the economy stupid!' so might Louis XVI have said, 'It's the debt stupid!'

To some extent Louis XVI cannot be blamed for the situation he inherited in 1774 – a huge royal debt with massive interest repayments to be made and a system of taxation that was inadequate. However, he can be blamed for three things:

■ the decision to involve France in the American War of Independence which so exacerbated the problems;

■ the failure to see through measures to reduce other aspects of royal spending;

■ the failure to reform taxation.

However, he was not solely responsible. In all three failings, others should share some of the blame: the ministers, such as Turgot and Necker, who gave Louis what turned out to be bad advice; the members of his own family, such as Marie Antoinette and the Duc D'Orleans, who either added to his problems or actually worked against him at times; the aristocracy and clergy in the Parlement of Paris and the Assembly of Notables who failed to agree with or support royal policy. But it was Louis who was in charge, even if his active involvement fluctuated. It was Louis who accepted the advice, it was Louis who changed policy and dismissed ministers and it was Louis who failed to convince those who mattered to support his government's policies. I personally agree with Thomas Carlyle's judgement on Louis, that he was 'taciturn and irresolute' (stated in *The French Revolution: A History, 1837*). In the end, Louis XVI was forced to call the Estates General because he had failed to implement the reforms necessary to avoid the bankruptcy of the monarchy.

Throughout this book you will have noticed the words 'I' and 'my' appearing, for example 'My view …'. It's unusual to find an obviously personal opinion in textbooks. Normally the writer uses impersonal wording that hides the fact that he or she has actually made a judgement. The danger is then that the writer's judgement sounds as if it's the correct, unchallengeable truth when it's really only an interpretation, though based on evidence and plenty of reading. I have used 'I' here (and elsewhere in the book) to highlight issues where I've made a judgement between competing interpretations.

You'll also see 'contractions,' such as *It's* or *they'd* in this book instead of *It is* or *they would*. This is because contractions make easier reading even if you're not supposed to use them in examinations.

■ **Concluding your enquiry**

Review your completed flow chart and your accompanying notes.

Write a short explanation of why Louis was forced to call the Estates-General. Think about:

• What the crown's core problem was

• Why reform failed

• Why Louis could not get agreement for new taxes

• Were there any decisions which could have been avoided or which made the situation much worse?

Paris – centre of the Revolution

As the capital of France, Paris, and its people, was to have an enormous influence on the course of the French Revolution.

As you have already seen, food prices elsewhere in France were important to local law and order but in the case of Paris, royal government recognised that it was a matter of national importance. Back in the spring of 1774 Turgot's free market policies meant that grain prices were not controlled and a poor harvest resulted in prices doubling in Paris. The riots that broke out had to be put down by soldiers and it took hundreds of arrests and two public executions to completely restore calm. Louis' ministers understood that if the capital went hungry then the state itself was at risk.

For this reason, supplying food to the capital was given priority over anywhere else in a 100-mile radius around the city.

What Paris was like – a novelist's interpretation

The following extract is from the novel *Pure* by Andrew Miller. The protagonist Jean-Baptiste is being shown round the neighbourhood.

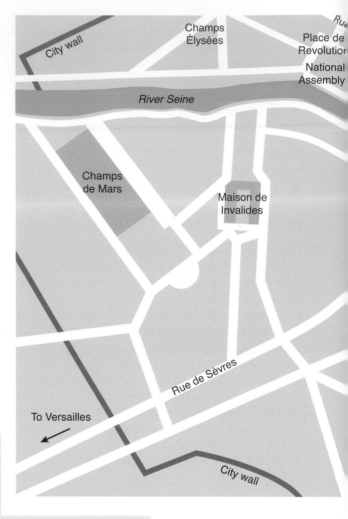

'Over there,' says the organist, waving an arm, 'you can eat well and cheaply. There on the corner, they'll mend your clothes without stealing them. And that's Gaudet's place. Gives a good shave, knows everyone. And here … here is the rue de la Fromagerie, where you can come when you want to breathe in something other than the perfume of graves. Go ahead. Fill your lungs.'

They have entered one end of a curious clogged vein of a street, more alley than street, more gutter than alley. The top stories of the buildings tilt towards each other, just a narrow line of white sky between them. On both sides of the street, every second house is a shop and every shop sells cheese. Sometimes eggs, sometimes milk and butter, but always cheese. Cheese in the windows, cheese laid out on tables and handcarts, cheese piled on straw, cheese hanging on strings or floating in tubs of brine. Cheese that must be sliced with a knife big enough to slaughter a bull, cheese scooped with carved wooden spoons.

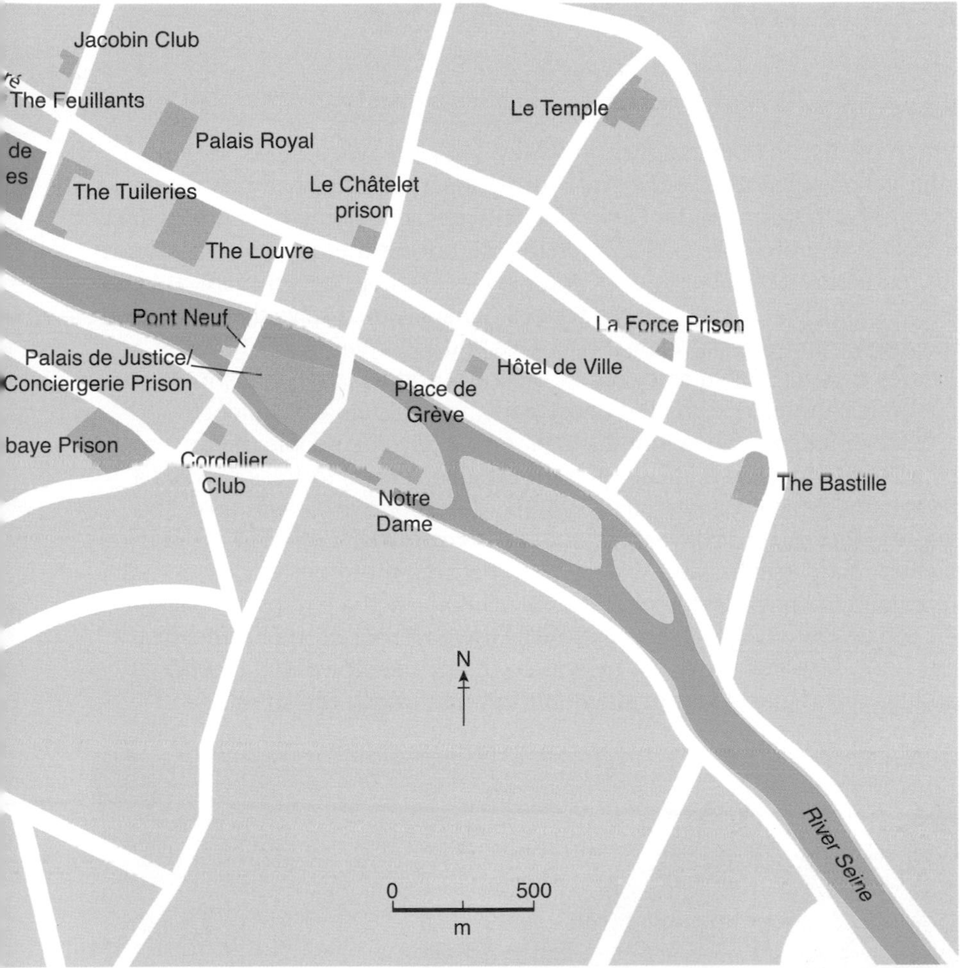

◁ Revolutionary Paris.

The following labels appear on the map:

Jacobin Club
The Feuillants
de
es
Palais Royal
The Tuileries
Le Châtelet
prison
Le Temple
The Louvre
Pont Neuf
Palais de Justice/
Conciergerie Prison
La Force Prison
Hôtel de Ville
baye Prison
Place de
Grève
Cordelier
Club
The Bastille
Notre
Dame
N
River Seine

0   500
m

◁ *The Port au Blé and the Port Notre-Dame*, painted by de Lespinasse in 1782. (See page 23 for an enlarged close-up.)

4 What sort of revolution took place in 1789?

sans-culottes
The name coined in 1791 for the small-property owners, shop keepers and workers, both masters and their employees, who came out in support of the Revolution. They were not the poor; in fact some were well off. Nor were they the rabble portrayed by their opponents. *Sans-culottes* translates as 'without breeches', the label suggesting they were trouser-wearing workers not bourgeois or nobles in silk stockings and breeches. Intriguingly after the Revolution they disappear as a group from French history.

When the Estates-General met on 5 May 1789 the two strands we have been following in Chapters 2 and 3 came together. Louis had been compelled to summon the Estates-General because of the continual failure to solve the crown's financial problems but once it met it provided a forum for discussion of the complaints and new ideas about government. If Louis and his ministers hoped that the Estates-General would solve their problems they were rapidly disappointed. Debates and arguments over how the Estates-General should carry out its business and which Estate should have the greatest influence created uncertainty, fear and finally, violence.

Only a little over two months later, on 14 July, the people of Paris, aided by soldiers, attacked and captured the Bastille, a royal fortress used as a prison and which was seen as a symbol of despotic royal authority. This was the first major involvement of the **sans-culottes**, the small-property owners, shop keepers and artisans who became the shock troops (provided the physical force) of the Revolution. By the end of the day over 90 people were dead. One of them was the governor of the Bastille (see page 45). After his surrender he was seized by the crowd and murdered and his bloody head was paraded in triumph through the streets.

▷ *Prise de la Bastille* by an anonymous artist. In the aftermath of the taking of the Bastille, Governor de Launay was murdered and his head carried through the streets on the head of a spike.

The key events of 1789

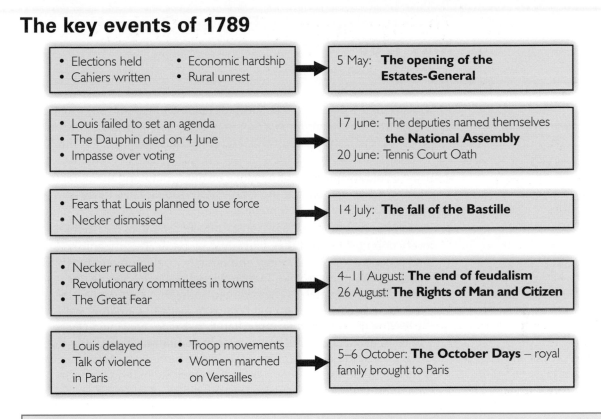

| • Elections held | • Economic hardship | 5 May: **The opening of the Estates-General** |
| • Cahiers written | • Rural unrest | |

• Louis failed to set an agenda	17 June: The deputies named themselves **the National Assembly**
• The Dauphin died on 4 June	20 June: Tennis Court Oath
• Impasse over voting	

| • Fears that Louis planned to use force | 14 July: **The fall of the Bastille** |
| • Necker dismissed | |

• Necker recalled	4–11 August: **The end of feudalism**
• Revolutionary committees in towns	26 August: **The Rights of Man and Citizen**
• The Great Fear	

| • Louis delayed | • Troop movements | 5–6 October: **The October Days** – royal family brought to Paris |
| • Talk of violence in Paris | • Women marched on Versailles | |

■ **Enquiry Focus:** What sort of revolution took place in 1789?

Events at the Bastille suggest that violence was an inevitable part of the Revolution from the beginning but is that true? And did the revolutionaries seek a complete end to monarchy or something more moderate? This chapter investigates what sort of revolution broke out in 1789 and particularly *how the nature of the revolution changed as events unfolded*. Completing this table will help trace those changes. After each section of the text on pages 40–49 fill in a row of the table with your overall conclusions and make detailed notes to justify your entry in each box.

	Aims Constitutional monarchy or a republic?	Methods Peaceful, threat of violence or actual violence?	Who were they? Peasants, *sans-culottes*, clergy, nobles, bourgeois?	Where events took place Paris, towns, rural France?
1. The opening of the Estates-General				
2. The National Assembly				
3. The fall of the Bastille				
4. The end of feudalism and the Rights of Man				
5. The October Days				

The opening of the Estates-General, May 1789

The Estates General had last met in 1614 so three questions about its organisation needed to be answered before it could open in 1789.

1. How were the deputies to be elected? Louis and his ministers agreed on a complex system for election that varied across France. Crucially this was free from royal control, and the government did not put forward any candidates.

2. How would the number of deputies be divided among the different estates? Louis agreed that the Third Estate should have twice as many deputies as the clergy and nobility.

3. Would the Estates vote by order or by head (one vote for each and every deputy)? In 1614 they had voted by order. This meant the First and Second Estates, the clergy and nobility, could outvote the Third Estate by two votes to one. To a growing number of people this was unfair and unacceptable. They wanted voting by head. Louis (on Necker's advice) left this to the Estates to decide when they met. By leaving the question for the Estates to decide, Louis and Necker hoped to avoid alienating one side or the other but in so doing made what proved to be a fatal mistake. If voting by head had been agreed in advance the Estates might have got on with debating a reform programme rather than challenging the power of the King.

The elections took place against a backdrop of economic hardship. The harvest of 1788 had been disastrous after a freak storm in July devastated crops across northern France. Elsewhere the harvest was poor due to a long spring drought. In addition the early months of 1789 were the harshest in memory with snow and ice destroying crops across northern France and frosts destroying the vines and olive trees in the south. As a consequence, food prices steadily rose (they reached their highest point on 14 July 1789) and people had to spend an ever higher percentage of their income on food, leaving little to spare. This in turn led to urban unemployment because there was a sharp fall in demand for industrial products.

When the voting ended the Estates-General was made up of the following:

- The voting system produced a First Estate that was dominated by parish priests rather than the bishops of the Church.

- In the Second Estate the voting system excluded new nobles whose status was not hereditary; and the traditional *nobles de court* were outnumbered by deputies from poor but longstanding noble families. The noble deputies tended to be conservative in their views, but there were 90 liberal nobles, a third of the noble deputies.

- In the Third Estate the system effectively excluded peasants and workers because deputies were initially not paid. The Third Estate deputies were therefore lawyers, landowners and office holders. There were also a few nobles and clerics who were not elected by their own estates so could stand for election as Third Estate deputies.

At the same time as the elections the three orders in each constituency were asked to draw up a list of grievances and suggestions for reform to guide the deputies. These were known as the *cahiers de doléances* (book of grievances). For the First Estate these suggestions included higher stipends, access to the higher offices of the Church, greater Church control of education and a limit to the toleration of Protestantism. The Second Estate was willing to give up its financial privileges but was split over whether to come to terms with the demands of the Third Estate which wanted to reform taxation and to have a modern constitution. All three estates wanted a king whose powers could be limited by an elected assembly which would have the power to raise taxes and pass laws.

One influential document was 'What is the Third Estate?', a pamphlet written by Abbé Sieyès and published in January 1789. In the first months of 1789, 30,000 copies were distributed. The extracts below show that already there were those who wanted radical political change. Sieyès demanded that the estates vote by head and not by order, arguing for the central importance of the Third Estate.

The plan of this work is quite simple. There are three questions that we have to ask ourselves:

1 What is the Third Estate? Everything.
2 What has it been until now in the existing political order? Nothing.
3 What does it want to be? Something. …

First we will see whether these answers are correct …

Who would dare to say that the Third Estate does not, within itself, contain everything needed to form a complete nation? It resembles a strong, robust man with one arm in chains. Subtract the privileged order and the Nation would not be something less, but something more. What then is the Third? Everything; but an everything that is fettered and oppressed. What would it be without the privileged order? Everything, but an everything that would be free and flourishing. Nothing can go well without the Third Estate, but everything would go a great deal better without the two others.

■ Now fill in the first row of your table. This stage is about the ideas being discussed and put forward.

Make more detailed notes which justify the summary in your table.

Such arguments and pamphlets had become common. According to William Doyle (2002) this '… was only the most eloquent among hundreds of no less vehement pamphlets denouncing the privileged orders …'

Emmanuel-Joseph Sieyès (1748–1836)

Sieyès was born into a bourgeois family and trained to be a priest for the Church. He was ordained in 1773 and served as secretary to the Bishop of Treguier. Influenced by the ideas of Rousseau (see page 24) and by the evidence of the problems he saw around him he became a supporter of reform. His influential pamphlet, 'What is the Third Estate?', brought him to political prominence in 1789 and he was elected as a deputy to the Estates-General. He was influential to begin with, drawing up the Tennis Court Oath and contributing to The Rights of Man. However, his opposition to the abolition of church tithes and belief in constitutional monarchy meant that his influence waned. Whilst he voted in 1793 for the execution of the King he kept a low profile during the Terror the following year. When asked afterwards what he had done during the Terror he replied, 'I survived.' After Robespierre's fall in 1794 he became influential once more and plotted the coup of Brumaire in 1799. Sieyès retired from public life after being outmanoeuvred by Napoleon who seized power for himself.

The deputies named themselves the National Assembly, June 1789

The Estates-General formally met at Versailles on 5 May. At this critical point Louis and his ministers failed to set the agenda. Louis was unsure what to do and lacked confidence in Necker, partly because Marie Antoinette and his brother Artois were so critical of his decision to accept Necker at all. So no programme of action was put forward for the deputies to discuss and no mention was made of a new constitution, something that all the *cahiers* had demanded. Necker talked of making taxation fairer but gave no details. So the initiative lay with the deputies and it was the Third Estate who took the initiative.

The three estates were to meet separately but the Third Estate argued that all deputies needed to have their election returns verified in a common session of all three estates together. Meeting together would set a crucial precedent for future discussions and create the likelihood of voting by head rather than by order. The nobility were against this and voted by 188 to 46 to meet as a separate order, as did the clergy, but by a much narrower margin, 133 to 114. Meanwhile the 580 deputies of the Third Estate refused to do anything until the other two orders joined them. For a month there was deadlock. Louis, mourning the death of his son the Dauphin on 4 May, was inactive.

Then came a vital week. On 10 June the Third Estate agreed to a proposal by Sieyès that they begin verifying deputies' credentials even if the other two estates did not join them. On 13 June the first three parish priests joined them, to great acclaim. In the following days a further sixteen priests joined and on 17 June the deputies of the Third Estate voted by 490 to 90 to call themselves the National Assembly. The importance of this was that they were claiming to represent the French nation. They also decreed that the collection of taxes should stop if they were dissolved. This claim to control taxation was a direct challenge to the King. Two days later the clergy voted by 149 to 137 to join the Third Estate, though not all did so immediately.

Faced with this challenge to his authority Louis tried to regain the initiative by holding a *séance royale* (Royal Session) attended by all three estates. The preparations involved the closure, without explanation, of the Third Estate's (now the National Assembly's) meeting room. Furious at what they saw as a despotic act the deputies moved to a nearby **tennis court** and took an oath, known ever since as the Tennis Court Oath:

> 'We swear never to separate ourselves from the National Assembly, and to reassemble wherever circumstances require, until the constitution of the realm is drawn up and fixed upon solid foundations.'

This was a critical moment. The National Assembly was claiming that Louis did not have the power to dissolve it. Just one deputy voted against. More clergy joined them and on 22 June the first two noble deputies did too!

As you can see on page 50 this was not a lawn **tennis court** but a court used for the game of 'real tennis'.

What would Louis say in the *séance royale*? He had three options.

2. Should I do what my younger brother the Comte d'Artois, my wife and other hardliners advise, and disband the National Assembly, by force if necessary? My Minister of War (Comte de Puységur) has on his own initiative reinforced the garrisons around Paris.

1. Do I adopt a conciliatory approach as Necker advises?

3. Or do I tell the deputies what I will and will not accept?

Louis chose the third option. He was still grieving over the death of his son and faced by the opposing arguments of Necker and Artois tried to steer a course somewhere in between. He offered some concessions on taxes but declared that the decrees of the National Assembly on 17 June were unacceptable to him and therefore void. After his departure the deputies were ordered to return to their separate rooms. As the Third Estate deputies wavered, one of them, the Comte de Mirabeau, took the lead saying, '… we shall not stir from our places save at the point of a bayonet.' When he heard this Louis reportedly said, 'Oh well, let them stay.'

In the following days, popular opinion turned against the privileged classes. There was rumour that Parisians were going to invade Versailles. In this climate Louis' hard-line advisers argued for a military solution. Meanwhile more clergy and nobles joined with the Third Estate in the National Assembly until by 27 June it numbered 830. At that point Louis ordered the remaining clergy and noble deputies to join the Third Estate deputies. A visiting Englishman, Arthur Young, said of the significance of Louis' decision, 'The whole business seems over, and the revolution complete.' Louis had a different view. He thought he was buying time to gather more troops around Paris.

Revolt in Paris – the fall of the Bastille, July 1789

In the last week of June, Louis took action and moved more troops into the Paris/Versailles area. These were **foreign** (Swiss and German), rather than French regiments. It was clear to all that he was planning to dissolve the National Assembly, using force if necessary. By the 11 July Louis had over 20,000 troops and this made him feel strong enough to dismiss Necker. Whilst Necker was very popular with the people Louis did not want to follow his reforming policies.

■ Now fill in the second row of your table. Does the rumour of an invasion by Parisians seem strong enough to be termed a threat of violence?

Make more detailed notes which justify the summary in your table.

The French army recruited Frenchmen but also had regiments made up of **foreign** mercenaries, in this case Swiss and German. Why do you think Louis moved these rather than French regiments?

43

When news of Necker's dismissal reached Paris on the 12 July it inflamed an already tense situation. High food prices in the city had triggered rioting and Necker was seen as the minister to solve the economic crisis. Meanwhile the King's opponents, those in favour of reforms, (both within and outside the National Assembly) were actively working against him through speeches, pamphlets and meetings, funded, it was said, by the Duc D'Orléans.

The trigger for armed revolt was the oratory of Camille Desmoulins, a pro-reform street speaker and pamphleteer, one of many funded by the Duc D'Orléans. He jumped onto a table outside the Café Foy in the garden of the Palais Royal to announce to the crowd that Necker had been dismissed. Apparently losing his stammer in his excitement, Desmoulins stirred the emotions of the people, calling on them to, '... take up arms and adopt cockades by which we may know each other' and claiming that a massacre of the supporters of reform was being prepared. He plucked leaves from a chestnut tree making green the colour for identifying the supporters of liberty. Drawing a pistol, Desmoulins declared that he would not fall into the hands of the police alive. The crowd hailed him as a hero and protectively carried him off.

People armed themselves by breaking into gunsmiths' shops. There were clashes with royal troops (German cavalry) in the **Tuileries** gardens, the hated **custom posts** around the city were attacked and there was looting and attacks on individuals. When the Gardes-françaises were ordered to withdraw from Paris many disobeyed and joined the people. That evening the **Paris electors** met to set up a citizen's militia drawn from the bourgeoisie to maintain order. Next day, the 13 July, barricades were set up to stop any more royal troops entering the city. Back in Versailles the National Assembly called for the removal of all troops from Paris.

Tuileries
A royal palace in Paris (see map on pages 36–37)

custom posts
Places which levied taxes on goods coming into the city

Paris electors
Men entitled to vote in elections for the Estates-General

Royal troops

Gardes-françaises – French regiment

Royal body guard – Swiss regiment

German cavalry

Revolutionary troops

National Guard, formerly citizen's militia

◁ Desmoulins' actions were originally commemorated by this statue but in 1941 the right wing French (Vichy) government which collaborated with Nazi Germany passed an order that inferior public works of art could be melted down for the war effort. The statue of Desmoulins was melted, as were statues of other revolutionary heroes Marat, Rousseau and Voltaire. Meanwhile over 8000 copies of the Marxist French historian Georges Lefebvre's *The Coming of the French Revolution* (1939) were ordered to be burned, a clear example of a regime trying to erase a history it found inconvenient.

On the 14 July 1789 the people of Paris seized control of the arsenal, Les Invalides, and took 28,000 muskets and 20 cannon. They still needed gunpowder and cartridges stored in the Bastille so they went there. The Bastille was a royal fortress and prison, a powerful symbol of royal power (see page 4). As the crowds massed around the Bastille royal troops in the city were withdrawn to the Champs de Mars, south of the River Seine. Their officers and commander knew they could not rely on their soldiers to fire on the crowds. Meanwhile at the Bastille the governor, de Launay, refused to hand over any gunpowder. At the time the crowd was not intending to attack but when a group got into the inner courtyard de Launay panicked and ordered his men to open fire, killing 93 people. The people, supported by the Gardes-françaises, then used cannon fire on the defenders of the Bastille. De Launay surrendered and was promptly murdered by the crowd and his head paraded through the streets on a pike.

△ In the early stages of the Paris revolt people wore red and blue cockades, the colours of Paris. To this Lafayette added the Bourbon white to give France the red, white and blue.

Those who stormed the Bastille were not the bourgeois middle classes who had led the protests against the monarchy but the *sans-culottes* (see page 38). Something like 250,000 Parisians were involved. This was the first and most famous of the *journées* which occurred during the Revolution.

Louis had lost control of Paris. His commanders told him that his troops could not be relied on to go into action in the city. On the 15 July, he and his brothers visited the National Assembly in Versailles to announce that he was withdrawing all troops from Paris and Versailles. In Paris the electors formed themselves into the new revolutionary council, the Commune, elected the deputy Jean-Sylvain Bailly as Mayor, turned the citizen's militia into the National Guard and appointed Lafayette as its commander. They were anxious to keep the *sans-culottes* under control.

journée
A day of popular action and disturbance linked to great political change

Louis now had to share his power with the National Assembly. He recalled Necker and on the 17 July visited Paris where he recognised the legality of the Commune and the National Guard. He even wore the red and blue cockade of the Revolution in his hat. The significance of this was not lost on others.

Amongst outside observers the British Ambassador wrote, 'The greatest revolution that we know anything of has been effected with … the loss of very few lives. From this moment we may consider France as a free country; the King a limited [that is, constitutional] monarch and the nobility as reduced to a level with the rest of the nation'.

The US commercial agent Gouverneur Morris wrote, 'You may consider the Revolution to be over, since the authority of the King and the nobles has been utterly destroyed'.

Meanwhile the Comte d'Artois, Louis's youngest brother, had left Versailles on his journey into exile. He clearly believed the royal cause was lost, as did the many other nobles who emigrated in the days and weeks ahead. One émigré who did not manage to leave was Bertier de Sauvigny, intendant of Paris. He and his father-in-law Foulon were seized by the crowds and accused of trying to starve the city. Without trial they were lynched from lanterns, decapitated and their heads (mouths stuffed with straw) paraded through the streets on pikes. The National Guard was powerless to prevent this.

■ Now fill in the third row of your table. Remember when you fill in the **Methods** column that it is the revolutionaries and not the King that you are looking at, even though Louis was clearly considering the use of violence.

What is the major change shown in your table?

The abolition of feudalism and the Declaration of the Rights of Man and Citizen, August 1789

July was not just a momentous month in Paris, but throughout France. Once Paris had acted, other towns felt confident enough to act. The Ancien Régime municipal corporations that ran towns were challenged for failing to deal with grain shortages. They were overthrown and replaced by revolutionary committees (in a few towns they worked alongside each other). This was frequently accompanied by violence. In Strasbourg the town hall was sacked. In Rouen grain stores were pillaged. So in the towns too the authority of the King was gone and the majority of his intendants abandoned their posts. These new revolutionary committees were composed of lawyers, property owners, and, in industrial centres, businessmen too, the bourgeoisie. Most towns set up a National Guard with twin objectives, to control the rioting and disorder and to prevent counter-revolution. In some places this had happened even earlier. In Marseilles in March a citizen's militia had been set up, and this was copied in other southern towns.

In the countryside unrest and violence had begun earlier. The bad harvest of 1788 had led to great hardship for the peasants as bread became expensive and scarce. In January 1789 there had been unrest in Franche-Comté which spread, in February, to Dauphiné and Provence. What began as sporadic attacks on grain storehouses and people who collected the feudal dues, by April had become more organised and targeted at landowners because peasants were suffering as grain shortages worsened. The calling of the Estates-General raised hopes and kept violence in check until July. Then news of the King's surrender and the defeat of the nobility were seen as a signal by the peasants to take action.

The Great Fear began, so called because of the panic amongst peasants due to rumours that gangs of brigands had been hired by fleeing aristocrats to take revenge by destroying the harvest. Peasants armed themselves and turned their attacks against the nobility. The hated symbols of feudal power, the bread ovens, dovecots and wine presses were destroyed. So too were the documents that recorded feudal obligations. Chateaux were burned but very few people, nobles or their agents, were killed. For example, in the Dauphiné généralité nine chateaux were burned, 43 pillaged and the archives of 13 destroyed.

News of the events in the countryside reached the National Assembly in Paris, causing great concern for the deputies. They wanted the rural revolt ended but did not want to call on royal troops to crush the peasants in case the King used the troops against the Assembly. Instead, the deputies decided to end the revolt and gain the support of the peasants by giving them what they wanted, the abolition of feudalism.

▽ The spread of the Great Fear.

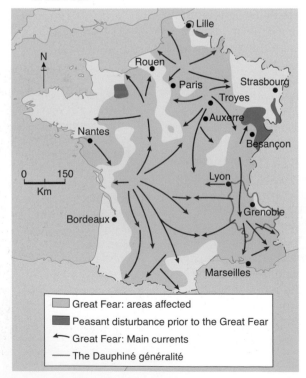

Great Fear: areas affected

Peasant disturbance prior to the Great Fear

← Great Fear: Main currents

— The Dauphiné généralité

The Deputies' plan was that on the evening of 4 August, when the assembly would be sparsely attended, a liberal noble, the Duc d'Aiguillon, would propose the abolition of aspects of feudalism such as feudal dues and labour services. But before he could speak, another noble, the Vicomte de Noailles, made his own proposals. Their two similar proposals changed the atmosphere in the Assembly. Deputies stepped forward in a patriotic fervour to give up one privilege after another. But old scores were settled too. Country nobles made sure that the courtiers lost their pensions and sinecures. The Bishop of Chartres proposed the abolition of the feudal right of hunting (beloved by nobles) whilst the Duc du Châtelet proposed the abolition of tithes. By the time the session ended at two in the morning the old order had been swept away. Étienne Dumont, an eyewitness, commented, 'A contagion of sentimental feeling carried them away'.

In the days that followed, the details behind the sweeping changes were debated, ending with the August Decrees published on 11 August. The Decrees declared that:

- feudal rights on people (serfdom) were abolished and those on property were to be replaced by a money payment
- tithes, hunting rights, *corveés*, seigneurial courts, venality of office, provincial and municipal privileges were all abolished
- all citizens were to be taxed equally
- all were eligible for any office in Church, state or army.

These decrees formally dismantled the Ancien Régime. The next task facing the deputies was to draft a constitution to replace it.

The first step was the Declaration of the Rights of Man and Citizen, published by the National Assembly on 26 August, a document of just 800 words. The deputies saw it as the basis for a new constitution. Its seventeen articles included the following extracts.

1. Men are born, and always continue, free …
2. Rights of man; … are liberty, property, security, and the resistance of oppression.
3. The nation is essentially the source of all sovereignty; …
4. Every man presumed innocent till he has been convicted, …
5. No man to be molested on account of his opinions, not even … religious opinions, …
6. … every citizen may speak, write and publish freely, …
7. Taxation … ought to be divided equally among the members of the community, according to their abilities.

Three days later the deputies passed a decree to re establish free trade in grain, a measure designed to keep the price of bread down.

■ Now fill in the fourth row of your table. In your notes make sure you provide detail of the changes to the Ancien Régime and assess how radical the Declaration was.

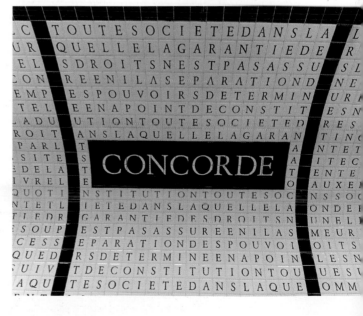

▽ Concorde Paris metro station line 12 is decorated with small ceramic tiles, each containing a single letter, which together spell out the Declaration of the Rights of Man and Citizen. What might this mural suggest about the French and their relationship with their history?

The October Days

The deputies who drafted the August Decrees and the Declaration of the Rights of Man and Citizen knew that they needed the agreement of the King. In a letter to the Archbishop of Arles Louis seemed undecided. On the one hand he praised, 'the first two orders of the state [the clergy and the nobility]. They have made great sacrifices for the general reconciliation, for their *patrie* and for their king'. However, he also wrote, '... I will never consent to the despoliation of my clergy and nobility ... I will never give my sanction to the decrees that despoil them, ...' Meanwhile the National Assembly debated whether the King should have the right to veto decrees. On 11 September it voted to allow the King a suspensive veto, where he could delay laws passed by the National Assembly for up to four years but not veto them completely. Clearly they were still intent on establishing a constitutional monarchy, not a republic.

In Paris, Louis' refusal to approve the August Decrees increased tension. Mayor Bailly and the Commander of the National Guard, Lafayette, were struggling to maintain law and order, especially as the price of bread, after falling in August, had risen again. The frequent bread shortages triggered riots. At the same time journalists like Desmoulins and Marat reported on the debates in the National Assembly and portrayed the supporters of a royal veto as unpatriotic and as not trusting the people. They called for unreliable deputies (those they disagreed with) to be purged, threatened aristocrats with lynching and advocated direct action by the people.

In this atmosphere of mistrust Louis took the decision to increase his protection by summoning the loyal **Flanders regiment** to Versailles. Their arrival gave him the confidence to write to the National Assembly to say that he would accept some, but not all, of the August Decrees. On the 4 October he also voiced his reservations about the Rights of Man.

The deputies felt betrayed by the King's actions and people all over Paris believed there was a counter-revolutionary attempt to starve the city. Rumours circulated of a banquet at Versailles to celebrate the arrival of the Flanders regiment which had resounded with unpatriotic songs and toasts and where revolutionary cockades were trodden underfoot. Holding a banquet in such hard times seemed a provocation in itself. On the morning of 5 October women from around the city marched to the **Hotel de Ville** and seized several hundred muskets and two cannon. The men of the National Guard made it clear they would not fire on the women. Then the women set off for Versailles in pouring rain shouting that they were coming for 'le bon papa', Louis. Seven thousand of them reached Versailles that evening and the deputies of the National Assembly had no choice but to welcome them. A deputation then went on to see the King and he was quick to agree to the August Decrees.

Louis now faced another decision. Should he fight or run away, choices suggested by **Saint-Priest** or should he stay, which Necker advised. In the end he decided it was his duty to stay but he sent his other brother, the Comte de Provence, to the safety of exile.

The **Flanders regiment** comprised French soldiers who had the reputation of being very well disciplined and reliable troops.

Hotel de Ville
Town hall (in this case, of Paris)

Francois, Comte de **Saint-Priest**, was a soldier and Minister in charge of the Royal Household.

◁ *A Versailles, a Versailles* the women's march on Versailles, an anonymous contemporary print.

Later that evening Lafayette and 20,000 National Guardsmen arrived in Versailles, having marched in the rain after the women. Lafayette tried to calm the explosive situation and asked the King to return to Paris with the people, which was what the National Guard wanted. The next morning (6 October) the crowd broke into the palace and were fired on by Swiss Guards acting as royal bodyguards. Two Swiss guardsmen were killed, their heads paraded on pikes, and the Queen narrowly escaped capture, perhaps murder, before the National Guard took control of the situation. Lafayette stopped the killing of any more Swiss guards and protected the royal family. He persuaded the King to appear on a balcony and announce he would come to Paris. Later that day the King and Queen and their family were escorted in their carriage back to Paris by the National Guard and by the people. With them went the deputies of the National Assembly.

The result of this second *journée* was that both King and National Assembly were forced to stay in Paris, so putting them in the power of the people of the city. It had been just five months since the Estates-General had met but in those five months the political system of France had changed dramatically.

■ Now fill in the final row of your table. In your detailed notes think about whether the King's actions had been a response to violence or had caused more violence.

■ Concluding your enquiry

Look back over your completed table and notes.

1 How much did the aims of the revolutionaries change?

2 When did violence develop and why did it increase?

3 Who was the driving force behind the Revolution – peasants, clergy, nobles, bourgeoisie, *sans-culottes*?

4 To what extent was this a Parisian revolution?

5 What sort of revolution was taking place at different times during the year?

6 Write a brief answer in about 250 words to the question: 'What sort of revolution took place in 1789?'

7 Historians have suggested different dates for the outbreak of the Revolution. Which would you choose – 17 June, 14 July, or 6 October – or another date?

Insight

David's painting *The Tennis Court Oath* (*Le Serment du Jeu de Paume*)

This is one of the iconic paintings of the Revolution. But is this painting useful evidence for us as historians of the Revolution?

Jacques-Louis David began work on it in March 1790. He was not there on the day but visited Versailles and made sketches, including of the tennis court. He jotted down ideas, 'remember to show the deputies moved to tears and holding their hands to their eyes', 'some serious and frowning, some laughing as if filled with delight, some respectful, some looking fiercely patriotic'; and 'Mirabeau, great energy, strength, vehemence, Sieyès, depth, Barnave, calm.' This research fed into the painting.

However, David was not a neutral observer. He wanted to encapsulate the heroic and united quality of the delegates and the event and so he used artistic license. He lowered the ceiling to give the figures greater prominence. The deputies are grouped as one whole and brought to the foreground so that individuals are recognisable. Martin Dauch, who refused to swear the oath, is seated far right, arms crossed and head bowed.

Edmond Dubois-Crancé is shown prominently in the right of the foreground standing on a chair with Gérard (praying), Mirabeau and Barnave around him. In front of them stands Robespierre, hands clasped to his chest in an expression of sincerity. Placed centrally standing on the table leading the oath is Bailly, whilst seated by it is Abbé Sieyès. Front and centre are a trinity of clergy, the Capuchin monk Dom Gerle, a parish priest Abbé Grégoire, and the Protestant Rabaut Saint-Etienne. Their mutual embrace symbolises the new united society, though Dom Gerle was not actually there on the day. Far left the octogenarian Père Gérard (a Breton noble who liked to dress up as a peasant) serves to link young and old.

Above the deputies there is further symbolism. A thunderstorm is indicated by clouds, an umbrella blown inside out and the storm driving the billowing curtains and the winds of liberty into the empty space at the centre of the room. A bolt of lightning flashes across the sky in front of the royal chapel. The union of politicians and people, young and old is enhanced by the spectators at the windows, including National Guardsmen and children.

One figure at the windows facing away is Marat. He is behind a soldier, writing. David was a great admirer of Marat and his newspaper, *Friend of the People*, but Marat had not been there either. In the bottom left of the gallery are more soldiers armed with muskets and a *sans-culotte* wearing the revolutionary symbol, a Phrygian cap. And in a nod to the usual use of the building, David has added a racket and balls front left.

As historians we could discount the painting as marred by inaccuracy but it does capture the heady early days of Revolution. However, it was never finished. David had begun the painting in 1791 but soon slowed down and gave up in September 1792. Events had overtaken him. Some central figures such as Bailly, Barnave and Mirabeau were no longer revolutionary heroes but traitors in disgrace, in prison or dead. To continue would have been dangerous for David himself.

5 What caused the French Revolution?

This short chapter brings together the themes developed in Chapters 2–4 and gives the opportunity to discuss the causes of the Revolution. Chapter 2 introduced a range of developments and problems in society that were creating criticisms of the Ancien Régime. Chapter 3 examined the pathway of events that forced Louis to call the Estates-General and Chapter 4 has described how, once the Estates-General met, events moved very swiftly and revolution began. It was, however, still a 'moderate' revolution in that the aim of the revolutionaries was to create a constitutional monarchy in which the King retained some degree of power. There was as yet no thought of creating a republic or executing the King.

■ Enquiry Focus: What caused the French Revolution?

One major component of studying history – and one of its wider values – is exploring and understanding why events take place. We begin by identifying causes or causal factors, then we look to see how they are connected and finally we try to make a judgement on which were the most important. That process is what this task is about.

Royal finances and the failure of financial reforms	Poverty in countryside and towns	The Enlightenment
The American War of Independence	Harvest quality and food prices 1788–89	The rise of the Bourgeois
Resentment over the tax system and corruption	The character and actions of Louis XVI	The decisions of the Assembly of Notables and the Parlement of Paris

1 Create your own set of cards with the headings above. Below the heading on each card summarise the part each factor played in the outbreak of revolution. Try to do this in just two or three sentences for each.

   To do this use your notes from chapters 2–4, then read this chapter to see whether you wish to add to or amend your summaries.

2 What different kinds of categories can you split the cards into?

3 What links can you see between any two or more factors?

4 Arrange the cards into a pattern (such as the Diamond 9 pattern) to explain why the Revolution broke out. For example, you could place the factor you consider the most important at its tip and the rest arranged below to show their relative importance, and how they are related.

5 a) How do you think each of the historians discussed on pages 55–56 would arrange these cards?

   b) Why would their patterns differ?

Balancing long- and short-term causes

Why did this revolution begin? Historians have examined a wide range of causes, from the very long-term developments through the eighteenth century to the immediate events of 1789. One example of a longer-term factor is the Enlightenment which has been identified as the starting point for a study of the French Revolution in many history books. To some historians it was one cause of the Revolution; to right wing historians it was <u>the</u> cause. These historians, from Burke onwards, argue that the Ancien Régime was stable and could have continued but that it was undermined by the Enlightenment. The most extreme claim is that the Enlightenment was a plot to promote atheism and anarchy. Other historians have argued that whilst the *philosophes* were certainly critics of the Ancien Régime they were not advocating revolution. There is disagreement amongst historians about how widely read Rousseau's works were before the Revolution, although some leading revolutionaries, such as Robespierre and Madam Roland, were influenced by his ideas.

At the other end of the argument is the view that the Revolution owed far more to more immediate events – increases in the price of bread, unemployment and hunger. In 1788–89 the price of grain was very high due to a bad harvest and there was a shortage of food. In the towns unemployment was rising because of falling demand for products and wages remained low as the price of bread went up. The winter was a particularly bad one. Most of a labourer's wages was spent simply on bread with little to spare even for wine to ease life's hardships. The situation was no better in the countryside where food riots took place in spring 1789 and grain stores were pillaged. But what if there had been good harvests, low food prices and less unemployment – would a revolution have taken place in the same way in 1789?

Somewhere between these extremes of long- and very immediate short-term causes lie a range of factors such as the role of the royal family and Louis XVI in particular. At a time of national crisis decisive leadership was needed but this was something Louis was unable to give. As you have already seen he failed to impress people and was regarded as a figure of fun by the aristocrats at his own court. An incident at the opening of the Estates-General illustrates his lack of presence. After a brief and uninspiring

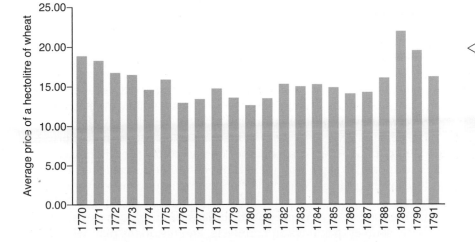

◁ National average price in livres of a hectolitre of wheat between 1770 and 1791. (From *The Longman Companion to the French Revolution* by Colin Jones, Pearson Education Limited © Longman Group UK Limited 1988.)

opening speech, he doffed his hat as a salute to the assembled deputies. After a royal wave he replaced his hat and then, after a respectful moment, so did the noble deputies. But then so did the Third Estate deputies, either because they had no idea of the correct etiquette that they should not wear a hat in the presence of the King or because they were following the lead of others out to cause trouble. In the confusion that followed some took their hats off again whilst others kept them on. Then Louis took his hat off again. The taking off and putting on of hats turned a solemn ceremonial occasion into a farce.

Moreover, during the opening days and weeks of the Estates-General Louis went through periods of political inactivity, going hunting or drinking instead of meeting ministers. This meant that ministers could do nothing. Some suggest Louis was depressed. Certainly he was disappointed by the failure of the Assembly of Notables and grief stricken by the death of the Dauphin on 4 June. Into the vacuum left by Louis moved the hard-liners in the royal family, his wife Marie Antoinette and his youngest brother the Comte d'Artois. They worked against Necker and any moves to make concessions. They were instrumental in the dismissal of Necker which was to precipitate the events of the 14 July 1789 when the Bastille fell.

Meanwhile, another member of the royal family who you have already met, Philippe, Duc D'Orleans was actively working against Louis but from a different standpoint. At the ceremonial opening of the Estates-General, Orleans deliberately walked amongst the deputies of the Third Estate. His Paris home, the Palais Royal, became a base for the **patriot party**. Orleans funded and protected the journalists and agitators like Desmoulins who attacked Louis' government. Their pamphlets could be published uncensored at his home. As Grand Master of the French Masonic order he was also closely linked to those masonic lodges where politics was discussed. Just how important his role was in bringing revolution is debatable; but that he contributed to it is certain.

These paragraphs have set the scene for the discussion that follows, tracing the ways in which historians have analysed the causes of the French Revolution.

patriot party
This was the name for all those who supported the new ideas in 1789

■ Use the discussion above to revise your factor cards. The absence of discussion of some factors above does not mean they were necessarily less important.

Are you a royalist, a liberal or a Jacobin? Historians and the causes of the French Revolution

The French historian François Furet in his introduction to *Interpreting the French Revolution* (1978) commented that as soon as a historian writes about the French Revolution they are 'labelled a royalist, a liberal or a Jacobin.' He was referring to the heated debates amongst historians about both the causes and the course of the French Revolution. We'll come to the course of the Revolution later but for the moment we will stick with its causes.

The debates about the causes of the Revolution began soon afterwards and still continue. There are a number of reasons for the differing interpretations. To begin with there is the nature of the evidence. Historical evidence is fragmentary, incomplete and sometimes contradictory.

Secondly, there is the methodological approach of the historian. There are different types of evidence that historians can use, such as written or statistical sources, paintings and artefacts; and historians may select from

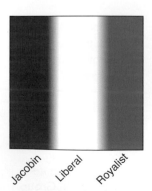

Jacobin Liberal Royalist

the extensive range of evidence that survives from the French Revolution. Moreover, historians have different interests and this may lead them to ask different questions. Are they interested in political, social, economic and cultural approaches, issues of gender and class, **history from below**, the use of local history, biography and the role of the individual? And what sort of history do they want to write, narrative or analytical, and for what audience?

Thirdly, there are the historian's own views on human society and the past, and the role of theory, such as Marxism, in their work. And finally, historians do not work in a vacuum. They are influenced by the political, social, economic and cultural climate of their own times.

Initially there were two positions on the French Revolution; those historians on the political right who were against the Revolution and those on the left who were for it. Then the problem of the violence in the Revolution split the latter group into two. The three viewpoints that then resulted are the right or Royalist; the centre or liberal; and the left or Jacobin or Marxist.

To the historians on the political right the Ancien Régime was still stable and viable in 1789. Therefore it was attacked from the outside, by the Enlightenment. At its most extreme this viewpoint saw the Enlightenment as a deliberate plot to overturn the social order, including the Catholic Church. This view became the orthodox position in France when it was ruled by the **Vichy** government, 1940–44. After that government fell and was discredited, so too was this interpretation for a time.

To the historians on the political left the Revolution was all about the heroic people overthrowing the repressive Ancien Régime and establishing a republican and egalitarian regime in its place. The Marxist viewpoint emerged in the twentieth century. The classic Marxist interpretation of the causes of the French Revolution is of a rising bourgeoisie, empowered by an emerging capitalist economy, denied political influence by the landed aristocracy. This school of historians, most notably Georges Lefebvre, developed the view that the Revolution was the result of the newly emerging bourgeoisie who were struggling to gain political power to match their commercial and capitalist power. The growing numbers of rich bourgeois merchants and industrialists therefore challenged both monarchy and aristocracy and in so doing made a revolution. This interpretation was challenged by non Marxist historians in the late 1950s but a modern historian still defending that view is Colin Jones. In *Bourgeois Revolution Revivified. 1789 and Social Change* (1991) he argued that the French economy was growing in the eighteenth century, with commercial trade growing dramatically by as much as 400 per cent and manufacturing more slowly by perhaps 75 per cent. He identified the cities that were strong revolutionary centres such as Paris, Lyons, Bordeaux and Marseilles as being the ones whose economies were growing fastest. And he argued that the increasing number of bourgeoisie resented the power of the old order and that prompted them to rebel.

To historians in the political centre the Revolution was justified by the abuses of the Ancien Régime. As with the left, this viewpoint saw the newly emerging bourgeoisie struggling against the monarchy and aristocracy as the main reason for the Revolution. Both emphasised the social and economic causes of the revolution. Where they differ the most is over the Terror (see page 94). Those on the left see it as necessary to the survival of the Revolution whilst those in the centre explain the Terror as being the Revolution being blown off course.

The **'history from below'** approach emphasises the importance of studying the lives and experiences of common people rather than political leaders and 'great men'.

Vichy
The right wing French Government which collaborated with Nazi Germany

Revisionists

These three positions framed debates about the Revolution until the middle of the twentieth century.

- In 1954 a revisionist interpretation was put forward by Alfred Cobban. He studied the revolutionary deputies in the Estates-General and identified that few of them were bourgeois capitalists. Instead he categorised them as lawyers and office holders and judged that the Revolution did not overthrow feudalism. Instead it was in fact a victory for the 'conservative, propertied, landowning classes'.

- Another historian, George Taylor (1964) made a similar categorisation but reached a different conclusion. He saw the nobles and bourgeoisie as having similar interests and being part of a single elite. But for him the Revolution was an accident that could have been avoided by a more able monarch than Louis. Today this view, that it was not so much a social conflict but more a political accident, is also argued by William Doyle (2002).

- Meanwhile François Furet (1970) argued that the causes were not social, were not a clash between rising bourgeoisie and aristocracy, but rather a constitutional crisis that paralysed the monarchy.

Post revisionists

By the late 1980s the term post revisionist was being used to describe a viewpoint that the Revolution was actually a symptom of deeper trends in French society such as the emergence of public opinion, **desacralisation** of the monarchy or the marginalisation of women in public life. Timothy Tackett (1996) studied the deputies in the Estates-General and argued that the nobility were wealthier and socially more advantaged than the deputies from the Third Estate. However, most nobles were less well educated than the deputies and four-fifths had military experience. So Tackett, whilst disagreeing with the Marxist interpretation, believes that social factors are important and that the nobility and bourgeoisie did not form a single elite.

desacralisation
No longer seen as being sacred

Micro history

The historian Peter Jones, in his book *Liberty and Locality in Revolutionary France: Six villages compared 1760–1820* (2003), adopted a 'micro history' approach. In the introduction he commented on his methodology, on his choice of these six villages:

'The case studies on which this book is based are not representative, therefore. Yet nor are they palpably unrepresentative. In a context of a little over 40,000 rural parishes at the end of the ancien régime, it would not have made much difference if I had studied sixteen, sixty or six hundred villages'.

He believes his micro approach, studying the detailed lives of all those in the six villages, allows him to generalise on rural society across France. So in terms of looking for long-term economic causes in the evidence of the peasant *cahiers* he argues that the '*cahiers de doléances* are best understood as blurred snapshots of a fleeting moment ...'. As you might expect his view of the Revolution from the perspective of the peasantry at a local level over a 60-year period is going to be very different from that of say Timothy Tackett who studied the deputies in the Estates-General in a single year, 1789.

■ Use the discussion of historians' views above to reflect on what you have written on your factor cards and particularly to help you with tasks 4 and 5 on page 52.

The Black Swan

In his book, *The Black Swan* (2007), the essayist and scholar Nassim Nicholas Taleb characterises some events as Black Swans. These are events that could not have been predicted at the time because they are so far outside of expectations. Based on his criteria which are listed below and what you know so far about Ancien Régime France, do you think that the French Revolution could be characterised as a Black Swan?

- The event is a surprise (to the observer).
- The event has a major impact.
- After the event, it is rationalised by hindsight, as if it could have been expected.

Is this the only book I should read?

No! No one book is sufficient to cover any major event in history and this one is no exception. You need to read others. I'd suggest five more history titles:

- *The Longman Companion to the French Revolution* (1988) by Colin Jones has sat on my desk for the past two years. Given a choice between this book or access to the internet to consult on the Revolution whenever I'm unsure about something I would pick this book every time. It contains a fascinating and quite amazingly comprehensive guide to the people and events of the French Revolution and all sorts of useful detail on any subject you can imagine from *abbé* (a title given to all clerics) to *visites domiciliares* (house to house searches for arms and suspects during the Terror).

- *Conspiracy in the French Revolution* (2007) edited by Peter Campbell, Thomas Kaiser and Marisa Linton is a collection of stimulating essays, written by some of the leading academic historians of the French Revolution today and will give you a real flavour of what a dynamic and relevant subject history can be.

- *Oxford History of the French Revolution* (2nd edition 2002) by William Doyle is authoritative, well written and highly detailed.

- *The French Revolution 1787–1804* (2nd edition 2010), by Peter Jones is a very popular undergraduate text. This offers a very succinct account and analysis of what happened and why, and includes a selection of key contemporary documents.

- *A New Dictionary of the French Revolution* by Richard Ballard (2011) is the sort of book you can dip into at any time and emerge with a fascinating snippet of information.

If you would like a fictional introduction to France in 1785 then the Costa Book of the Year 2012 *Pure* by Andrew Miller is an excellent read. One reviewer wrote: 'Reading it, you feel as if you are in Paris before the Revolution, a city at once decaying and on the cusp of momentous change, a place of disgusting smells and odd subcultures, at once recognisable and utterly foreign.'

How did people in Britain react to the Revolution?

> It was the best of times, it was the worst of times, it was the age of wisdom, it was the age of foolishness … it was the spring of hope, it was the winter of despair …

These words come from the opening lines of the most famous novel set during the French Revolution, *A Tale of Two Cities* by Charles Dickens, published in 1859. They capture both the variety and the extremes of reactions felt by people in Britain to the news of developing events in France.

There were certainly those who saw the early days of the Revolution as 'the best of times'. The scientist Erasmus Darwin wrote to James Watt hailing the dawn of 'universal liberty', saying 'I feel myself becoming all French in chemistry and politics'. The industrialist, Josiah Wedgwood, spoke of 'the wonderful revolution' and set about manufacturing thousands of souvenir pottery medallions to celebrate the fall of the Bastille. The romantic poet William Wordsworth, who visited France in July 1790, wrote in his autobiographical poem *The Prelude*:

> Bliss was it in that dawn to be alive,
> But to be young was very Heaven!

Politicians too were initially enthusiastic. Charles James Fox declared the Revolution to be 'much the greatest event that ever happened in the world'. The Prime Minister, William Pitt, hoped that the French would, like the British, now live under a constitutional monarchy. To many Britons it seemed that the French were simply catching up with the superior British system of government.

However, as violence increased, critics of the Revolution became more vociferous. In November 1790, an MP, Edmund Burke, published a pamphlet, *Reflections on the Revolution in France*, condemning the Revolution. While Burke was not against change and believed that people had the right to depose a despotic government he criticised the developing violence and argued for gradual change by constitutional means and for the protection of property and the Church. He believed the Revolution was the result of a conspiracy by the 'moneyed interest' anxious to gain status and profits and more importantly by philosophers of the Enlightenment committed to destroying Christianity. He warned that a political doctrine founded upon abstract ideas such as liberty and the rights of man could easily be abused to justify tyranny. He predicted that:

> … some popular general, who understands the art of conciliating the soldiery, and who possesses the true spirit of command, shall draw the eyes of all men upon himself. Armies will obey him on his personal account … the moment in which that event shall happen, the person who really commands the army is your master.

Burke may have been thinking of Lafayette but his prediction came true when Napoleon seized power in 1799.

Burke's pamphlet, a best seller, sold 30,000 copies in two years but sparked a number of responses, most famously *The Rights of Man* by Thomas Paine in 1791. Paine played down Burke's criticisms of the savagery of the Revolution by giving a precise account of the storming of the Bastille and the October Days and highlighting the achievement of the revolutionaries in drawing up the Rights of Man and Citizen. He argued that the British should follow suit and abolish nobility, titles and the monarchy. Sales of this pamphlet were even more spectacular, about 200,000. Stimulated by events in France and by Paine's arguments, reform clubs sprang up across Britain, campaigning for political reforms which would create a fairer electoral system including giving ordinary working men the vote.

These two pamphlets represented the diversity of reactions captured by Dickens in *A Tale of Two Cities*. On one side, encouraged by the ideals of the Revolution (though not by the violence) were those who wanted political change in Britain. On the other side were the reactionaries who opposed change and feared that even peaceful protests were the beginning of revolution and widespread blood-letting. The outbreak of war between Britain and France in 1793 increased this fear and led to the government banning public meetings of more than 50 people and the arrest and transportation of some reform club leaders.

This debate between those who saw the Revolution as a time of hope and those who saw it as reason to despair continued in Britain for the next 30 years and beyond. Whenever ordinary people marched to demand the right to vote (as at Peterloo in 1819 or during the Reform crisis of 1830–31), the government sent in soldiers to break up the protests on the grounds that this was preventing a revolution. Therefore, the influence of the French Revolution on Britain did not end in 1798 or 1815 but continued to reverberate through British politics throughout the first half of the 1800s.

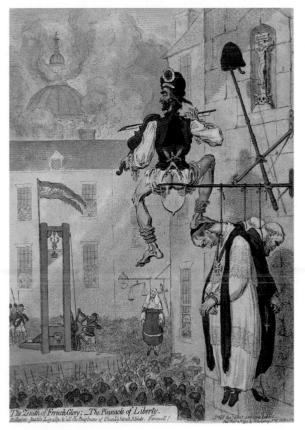

▷ *The Zenith of French Glory: the Pinnacle of Liberty, Religion, Justice, Loyalty & all the bugbears of Unenlightened Minds Farewell!* by James Gillray, etching with hand colouring, 1793. Once war broke out between France and Britain, the characterisation of the French revolutionaries as bloodthirsty savages gained ground. Here Gillray shows the *sans-culotte* sitting on a lamp bracket, his foot on the head of one of the hanging churchmen. He fiddles whilst in the background the church burns and in the foreground Louis XVI is guillotined. The watching crowd are shown with revolutionary bonnets.

Revolutionary changes

1. Who was governing France from 1790?

Louis XVI remained King until his deposition in August 1792.

Between 1789 and 1795 there were three representative assemblies. These were:

1 The **Estates-General** which first assembled on 5 May 1789. This later renamed itself the **National (Constituent) Assembly** and sat until 30 September 1791. Its deputies were originally interested in making reforms to the existing political system, that is the monarchy, but became more radical as events unfolded.

2 Following elections in 1791 the **Legislative Assembly** assembled on 1 October 1791 and sat until 20 September 1792. Its deputies were divided between those who wanted a constitutional monarchy to work and those who did not.

Louis was deposed as King by the *journée* of 10 August 1792. There was then a period of transition lasting until 20 September 1792 when power was in the hands of three groups – the Legislative Assembly, the Provisional Executive Council and the Insurrectionist Committee or Commune.

The **Provisional Executive Council** was a provisional form of government with six ministers headed by Danton, who was Minister for Justice, and Roland who was Minister for the Interior.

The **Insurrectionist Committee** or **Commune** was the committee, dominated by the *sans-culottes*, that plotted and carried out the overthrow of the monarchy.

3 This period of transition ended with the third representative assembly, the **National Convention**, which first assembled on 20 September 1792 and stayed sitting until 26 October 1795. The deputies elected to this body were committed to the new republic. During this period a key group at the centre of government was the Committee of Public Safety led by Robespierre.

From November 1795 to November 1799 France was governed by the Directory, a moderate democratic government, steering a middle way between a reintroduction of the monarchy on the right and the introduction of a popular democracy on the left. The National Convention continued as the elected legislature.

In November 1799 the Directory was overthrown by Napoleon Bonaparte (the head of the army, see page 122). Napoleon now ruled France and within two years was elected Consul for life.

Estates-General became:

- **National (Constituent) Assembly** from 1789–September 1791
- **Legislative Assembly** from October 1791–September 1792
- **National Convention** from September 1792–October 1795

2. What were the main political groups between 1790 and 1795?

The range of revolutionary groups can appear complex as people's views changed as the Revolution progressed and so men and women left one group to join another. That said, we can crudely divide people up into three main political groups – the **Feuillants**, the **Girondins**, and the **Jacobins**.

The **Feuillants** group were constitutional royalists. Amongst its leading figures were Barnave and Lafayette. They wanted to make constitutional monarchy work and were in control of the National Assembly in August and September 1791 and influential until early 1792.

The **Girondins** group can be loosely described as more moderate revolutionaries. They came to be known as Girondins because some of the deputies in the group represented the Gironde department of France. Amongst its leading figures were Brissot and the Rolands. They were pro war, in favour of a republic, and very influential in the National Convention until they were purged in the *journée* of 2 June 1793 by their enemies, the Jacobins.

Both the Feuillants and Girondins were originally **Jacobins** but they left (or were expelled). The remaining group of Jacobins can be loosely described as more extreme revolutionaries who demanded the execution of Louis XVI to safeguard the Republic. They were also known as Montagnards (see page 79). Amongst its leading figures were Danton and Robespierre. They held power from 1793 until the overthrow of Robespierre in the Thermidor Coup.

Two smaller but also significant groups were the Hébertists and the Dantonists (or Indulgents).

The **Hébertists** were a left wing group gathered around the journalist Jacques-René Hébert who opposed the revolutionary government of the Committee of Public Safety and who agitated for greater social and economic reforms, an increase in the Terror and for de-Christianisation. They were guillotined in March 1794.

The **Dantonists** was the name given to the group guillotined with Danton on 5 April 1794 who had been calling for an end to the Terror.

3. The Revolutionary Calendar

As part of its break from the past, the National Convention voted on 5 October 1793 to adopt a new revolutionary calendar. This was backdated to begin with Year I of the new Republican era on 22 September 1792, the day after the abolition of the monarchy. The year was divided into 12 months, each of 30 days which were in turn divided into 10-day weeks, the final day of which would be a day of rest. The five supplementary days became known as *sans-culotides* and were national holidays. This calendar was a deliberate rejection of the Christian calendar and ignored Sundays and saints' days. Robespierre opposed this, believing that de-Christianisation alienated people from the Revolution. He wrote in his private notebook, 'indefinite adjournment of the decree on the new calendar'. Nevertheless it was passed and put into action, although it proved impossible to completely stamp out the observance of Sundays. The calendar survived until December 1805, when it was abolished by Napoleon.

Month	Meaning	Began
Vendémiaire	vintage	22 September 1792
Brumaire	mist	22 October
Frimaire	frost	21 November
Nivôse	snow	21 December
Pluviôse	rain	20 January 1793
Ventôse	wind	19 February
Germinal	seeds	21 March
Floréal	flowers	20 April
Prairial	meadows	20 May
Messidor	harvest	19 June
Thermidor	heat	19 July
Fructidor	fruit	18 August

6 Was Louis XVI chiefly to blame for the failure of constitutional monarchy?

constitutional monarch
A monarch whose powers are limited by a constitution

constitution
The fundamental principles according to which a state is governed which can be written as in the case of France or unwritten as in the case of Great Britain

A revolution had broken out but no one knew in 1789 what kind of revolution it would turn out to be. The majority of the deputies in the National Assembly expected a 'moderate revolution' – one in which the monarchy remained but with its powers reduced and shared with a wider range of the French people. This is what happened for two years because from the revolutionary events of October 1789 onwards France was effectively governed by a **constitutional monarch**. Louis was still king but was now subject to the law just like every other citizen of France. Laws were no longer made by the King but by the deputies sitting in the National Assembly. They were at work drafting a **constitution** intended to secure the future of the Revolution and the gains made. But could the deputies trust Louis to accept the constitution and become a constitutional monarch? The cartoonist who made this etching in 1791 thought not. He shows Louis XVI facing two ways. On one side Louis promises the National Assembly deputies that, 'I will support the Constitution.' And on the other hand he promises those clergy who have refused to swear an oath to the Constitution that, 'I will destroy the Constitution.'

The struggle to create an effective constitutional monarchy lasted for two years from autumn 1789 to autumn 1791. This struggle basically meant reaching agreement on how the country was to be governed. There were many questions that needed answering.

- Who would be allowed to vote?
- How would taxes be raised?
- Would Catholicism be the official religion of France?
- What powers would the King have? For example, would he be allowed to veto new laws?

Once the National Assembly had decided on the answers to these questions in September 1791 Louis accepted the new constitution. It appeared as if the problems had been solved but within two months Louis vetoed two new laws on key issues. At that point it was clear that the attempt to create a constitutional monarchy had failed. Was this all Louis' fault, as the cartoonist hinted, or should others share the blame?

◁ *Le Roi Janus ou l'homme à deux visages.*

The chronology of constitutional monarchy 1789–91

October 1789	Early co-operation between Louis and the deputies of the National Assembly. Louis agreed to the Declaration of the Rights of Man and Citizen and to the abolition of feudalism.
November 1789	The National Assembly nationalised all Church property but collaboration with the King was hampered by the decision to bar National Assembly Deputies from being royal ministers.
February to June 1790	The National Assembly passed a range of reforms: • France was reorganised into 83 departments, Paris into 48 sections. • Abolition of *lettres de cachet*, the *gabelle* and hereditary nobility.
April to June 1790	Counter-revolutionary uprisings in Nimes, Montauban, Toulouse and Vannes
July to August 1790	The National Assembly made more reforms – the Civil Constitution of the Clergy completely reorganised the Catholic Church in France, the legal system was also reorganised.
November 1790	As relations between the deputies and the King declined Louis began secret negotiations with other European countries. A National Assembly Decree ordered priests to take the oath to the Constitution.
February 1791	The political temperature was raised by the 'Chevaliers du poignard' conspiracy – the Tuileries were temporarily invaded by armed young nobles, counter-revolutionaries who may have been planning to abduct the King.
April 1791	Two events made a successful constitutional monarchy even less likely: • Mirabeau, whose influence with Louis many believed would make constitutional monarchy work, died • the people of Paris prevented the royal family from leaving for Saint-Cloud for Easter.
June 1791	The royal family failed in their attempt to flee to Varennes. All trust between the King and deputies had broken down.
July 1791	The emergence of the idea of Republicanism led to a split in the Jacobin Club. Pro-constitutional monarchists formed the Feuillant Club and took control in the aftermath of the Massacre of the Champ de Mars.
August 1791	In signs of deepening divisions a National Assembly Decree ordered all *émigrés* to return to France within one month whilst in the Pillnitz Declaration Leopold II of Austria and Frederick-William II of Prussia threatened a combined military intervention in French affairs on behalf of the French monarchy.
September 1791	Louis accepted the new Constitution and the National Assembly met for the last time.
October to November 1791	Brissot and his republican supporters in the new Legislative Assembly passed two laws directed against those clergy who refused to swear an oath of loyalty to the Constitution and against *émigrés* which led to Louis using his veto.

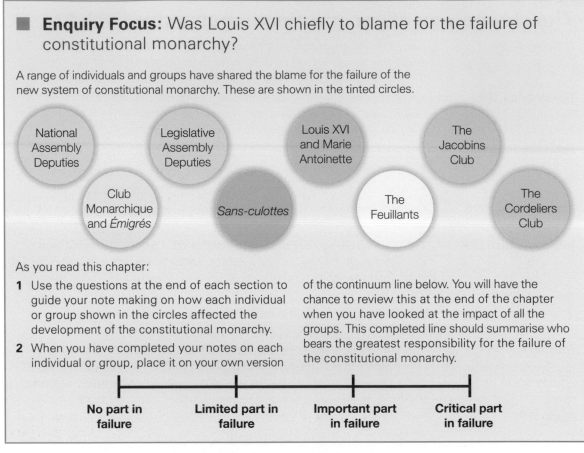

■ **Enquiry Focus:** Was Louis XVI chiefly to blame for the failure of constitutional monarchy?

A range of individuals and groups have shared the blame for the failure of the new system of constitutional monarchy. These are shown in the tinted circles.

National Assembly Deputies

Legislative Assembly Deputies

Louis XVI and Marie Antoinette

The Jacobins Club

Club Monarchique and *Émigrés*

Sans-culottes

The Feuillants

The Cordeliers Club

As you read this chapter:

1 Use the questions at the end of each section to guide your note making on how each individual or group shown in the circles affected the development of the constitutional monarchy.

2 When you have completed your notes on each individual or group, place it on your own version

of the continuum line below. You will have the chance to review this at the end of the chapter when you have looked at the impact of all the groups. This completed line should summarise who bears the greatest responsibility for the failure of the constitutional monarchy.

No part in failure

Limited part in failure

Important part in failure

Critical part in failure

The decisions of the deputies of the National Assembly

When Louis agreed to the Rights of Man and Citizen and to the abolition of feudalism in October 1789 many believed the Revolution was over. However, the National Assembly still had to reform how France was governed. Some of these reforms, such as those to taxation, addressed problems that Louis and his ministers had tried to solve, others such as creating a written constitution were more far-reaching. Most had widespread support from within the National Assembly and the general population.

Local government and the voting system

The deputies wanted to replace the administrative chaos of the Ancien Régime with a coherent structure. They also wanted to give more power to local areas and for the system to be democratic with all officials elected. This was because weakening the central government was one way to safeguard the Revolution as it made it more difficult for Louis to recover his power. Even at this early stage there were clearly deputies who did not trust Louis.

While more efficient administration was welcome to everyone, the degree of democracy planned for the new constitution was not enough for some while too much for others. Under the new system the right to vote in elections in communes (see the diagram) was open to all men over 25 who paid tax equivalent to 3 days' wages. This gave over 4 million Frenchmen the right to vote (they were known as 'active citizens'). However, it excluded nearly 3 million men and all women. They had no vote (they were 'passive citizens'). The deputies were unwilling to give power to the lower orders of society.

In addition, voting in elections at canton, department and National Assembly level was only open to those men paying tax worth 10 days' wages. To stand for election to be a deputy required a tax payment that was out of the reach of most Frenchmen. So the system was heavily weighted in favour of the wealthy. Robespierre was one deputy who spoke out against these measures whilst Camille Desmoulins wrote in his newspaper:

> But what is this much repeated word active citizen supposed to mean? The active citizens are the ones who took the Bastille.

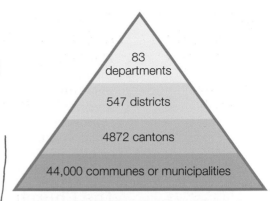

△ By a decree of February 1790 France was divided into 83 departments for elections and local government. Departments were divided into districts (547), cantons (4872) and communes or municipalities (approx. 44,000) which would be run by elected councils.

The new legal system

This also aimed to limit the power of the monarch. Ancien Régime features such as parlements, *seigneurial* courts and the hated *lettres de cachet* (see page 4) were abolished. They were replaced by a uniform system with a **Justice of the Peace** in each canton and a criminal court with trial by jury in each department. Torture and mutilation were abolished, anyone arrested had to brought before a court within 24 hours and a new and more humane method of execution, the guillotine, was approved. This replaced previous methods including decapitation (usually for nobles) and being broken on the wheel (for members of the Third Estate). Justice was made free and equal for all.

Justices of the Peace
JPs tried criminal cases up to the value of 50 livres. They were elected by active citizens and served for two years

Tax

Reforming the taxation system was more problematic. When royal government collapsed in 1789 the deputies tried to continue collecting taxes under the existing system until a new system was set up but people simply refused to pay and officials trying to collect taxes often faced physical threats. For example, in Picardy, income from indirect taxes fell by 80 per cent. Recognising the realities the deputies abolished the most unpopular indirect and direct taxes and the old system of tax farming.

The nationalisation of Church land provided an interim source of income. Bonds backed by the value of these lands, called **assignats**, were issued as 1000-livre notes. They were soon being used as paper money to pay the government's creditors and to buy more Church land. The deputies hoped this would safeguard the Revolution because those who bought land from the Church would have a vested interest in supporting the Revolution, as would the clergy who now received a salary from the state.

A new taxation system based upon citizens paying according to what they could afford, was introduced. There were just three taxes – the *contribution foncière*, a land tax which everyone had to pay; the *contribution mobilière*, a tax on moveable goods such as grain paid by 'active citizens'; and the *patente*, a tax on commercial profits. This was a fairer system.

assignats
Assignats were initially government bonds secured on the value of nationalised Church land. A buyer gave money to the government and in return received a bond which would pay interest. If the government needed to repay the bond holder then they could do so by selling some of the Church land. Over time *assignats* came to be used as a paper currency

Economy

The deputies believed in laissez-faire, that government should not interfere with trade and industry. So all internal customs barriers were abolished and price controls were removed. The old system of guilds (see page 23) which had restricted entry to crafts was also abolished. These reforms were previously attempted by Louis' ministers.

However, in one area of trade and industry, the deputies did intervene. When, in June 1791, thousands of workers in Paris were threatening to strike for higher wages the deputies passed the Le Chapelier Law which banned trade unions and employers' organisations. Strikes were made illegal.

The Church

It was when the deputies began reforming the Church that divisions within France, which threatened the successful working of constitutional monarchy, really began to appear.

- Abuses such as pluralism were abolished.
- Clergy were paid by the state instead of collecting the tithe.
- Monastic orders that did not provide either education or charitable work were suppressed.
- Civil rights were granted to Protestants in 1789 and Jews in 1791.

The clergy accepted all this. However, many were very unhappy when the deputies refused to make Catholicism the official religion of France. Matters came to a head in July. On 12 July 1790 the deputies approved the Civil Constitution of the Clergy. Dioceses were to coincide with the new departments, which reduced the number of bishops from 135 to 83. All other clerical posts apart from parish priests would disappear. The crucial clause was:

> From the publication of the present decree there will be only one way of appointing to bishops and curés, namely election.
>
> All elections will be conducted by ballot; the successful candidate will have an absolute majority of votes.

This brought the Church into conflict with the deputies. Elections were opposed by many of the clergy, although they wanted to find a way to accept the Civil Constitution. Their request for a national synod (council) of the French Church was rejected. The deputies refused to allow the Church a privileged position. Denied a synod, the clergy waited for the judgement of the Pope, Pius VI. He delayed and, growing tired of waiting, the deputies forced the issue by a decree on 27 November 1790 which required all clergy to take an oath to the Constitution. This split the Church. For many clergy the oath swearing 'fidelity to the nation, the law, the King and the Constitution' posed a potential conflict with their first loyalty to God. They saw it as a choice between their religion and the Revolution. The oath posed a crisis of conscience for Louis too. He delayed signing the legislation until 26 December 1790.

During January and February 1791 roughly 60 per cent of parish priests took the oath but only three bishops did so and when in March the Pope denounced the Civil Constitution some priests retracted. Finally about 50 per cent of parish priests swore the oath. Those who refused were known as **refractory clergy** and were removed from their parishes, although a shortage of replacements meant that some were asked to stay on. The removal of priests was very unpopular with parishioners. For the first time, a significant number of people were now opposed to the Revolution.

refractory clergy
Those clergy who refused to swear an oath of loyalty to the Constitution

Louis XVI

Louis had accepted the changes of 1789 and whilst he was not entirely trusted by the deputies, they were prepared to work with him to establish a constitutional monarchy. However, opinion amongst historians is divided on whether Louis was prepared to accept a constitutional monarchy. The historian Munro Price studied Louis' secret correspondence with **Mirabeau** and suggests in an article in 2006 that:

> Instead of *whether*, the key word should be *when*. From July 17, 1789, to the middle of 1790, most of the evidence points to the king's decision to collaborate sincerely with the Constituent Assembly. During that summer, however, his confidence in the assembly's deliberations collapsed.

1 This section has looked at five reforms made by the National Assembly, relating to the voting system, the economy, taxation, the legal system and the Church. For each reform note down whether it created support for, or opposition to, the new constitution and the reasons for its effects.

2 Now place National Assembly Deputies on your continuum line, adding brief notes to justify this placement.

What undermined Louis' confidence was the Civil Constitution of the Clergy (see above) and the realisation that his negotiating position was weakened as long as he was in Paris. When, in April 1791, Louis and his family tried to leave Paris to spend Easter at Saint Cloud a huge crowd blocked them in. When Lafayette ordered his National Guard to clear a path through the crowds his men refused. It was at this point that historians such as William Doyle believe Louis realised he was a prisoner in his own capital and that he needed to escape.

Mirabeau was a leading revolutionary in the National Assembly who was secretly advising the royal family.

Louis planned to escape from Paris to Montmédy in Lorraine where he could negotiate with the National Assembly deputies from a position of strength. In June, Mirabeau advised the King to leave Paris under military escort and warned, 'Remember ... that a king must leave in broad daylight if he wants to continue as a king.' Louis ignored this advice. On the night of the 20 June 1791 the King and the royal family, disguised as servants of a Russian aristocrat, secretly left the Tuileries. They travelled east in a large coach but were recognised and then stopped at Varennes. From Varennes they were brought back to Paris where the crowds greeted them with an ominous silence. Meanwhile the King's younger brother, the Comte de Provence, and his family did successfully escape to the Austrian Netherlands.

Before he left Paris, Louis had written a proclamation for the French people. In it he set out his true feelings and denounced the Revolution. He argued that it had gone against the wishes of the people set out in the *cahiers*, that the crown had insufficient power under the new constitution, that the power of the Jacobin Club was too great, that property had been attacked and that there was anarchy in parts of France.

The deputies of the National Assembly who had been working towards establishing a constitutional monarchy were appalled. Without the King their new constitution was worthless. To try and keep things on track, they declared

1 Make notes
which explain:
Louis' attitude to
constitutional
monarchy; which
issues most
influenced his
attitude; how his
actions created
mistrust and
opposition; the
impact of his
proclamation to
the people.

2 Now place Louis
XVI on your
continuum line,
adding brief
notes to justify
this placement.

Antoine **Barnave** was
a barrister and one of
the early leaders of the
Revolution. After
accompanying the royal
family back from
Varennes he worked
for the continuation of
constitutional monarchy
and was a leading
member of the
Feuillants. When they
failed, he returned to his
home region but was
arrested and guillotined
on 29 November 1793.

▷ A contemporary
cartoon showing the
royal family being
escorted back to
Paris by the National
Guard. Why has the
cartoonist chosen to
depict them as pigs?

that Louis had been kidnapped and was therefore blameless. No one believed this fiction. The key consequence of Louis' botched flight to Varennes was that people had to make a choice. Did they come out in support of constitutional monarchy or in favour of republicanism? The stream of *émigrés* increased with roughly 6000 army officers (all noble) and refractory clergy (see page 67) leaving France. Meanwhile, for many the monarchy was irretrievably damaged. In Paris, shop and inn signs which featured images of the King were destroyed by angry crowds. Most damaging of all was that many moderate politicians no longer believed that constitutional monarchy could work.

Marie Antoinette

The Queen's unpopularity increased further in this period. She became more active in politics, having secret discussions with Mirabeau and **Barnave** as they tried to make constitutional monarchy work, and she advised the King. She was never in favour of constitutional monarchy and described the Constitution of 1791 as 'monstrous'. She was blamed when Louis used his veto and was then nicknamed 'Madam Veto'. She also wrote many letters, some in code or lemon juice (which makes an invisible ink and turns brown when heated) and sent via trusted couriers, appealing to other European monarchs for military help. As the Comte de Mercy, Austrian ambassador to France since 1766, suggested in a letter to Mirabeau, changing the Queen's views was never easy.

The queen has a proud and decided character; her lack of education and knowledge sometimes leads her into wrongheaded opinions, to which she holds with a constancy that resembles obstinacy, but since she has some intelligence and discernment, it is possible, although difficult, to talk her out of these by force of reasoning; once this has been achieved, her position is certain to stay fixed. It is important to observe that only half convincing her is insufficient and can allow a return to her old prejudices …

Was she to blame for the downfall of the monarchy? One contemporary, the American Thomas Jefferson, was clear. 'I have ever believed that had there been no queen, there would have been no revolution.' A modern American, historian Thomas Kaiser (2000) differs, 'In recent years, feminist historiography has reconfigured the "Marie Antoinette question" in significant ways. The effect of this approach has been to place Marie Antoinette at the centre of systemic anxiety regarding the "unnatural" public power wielded by women in the late eighteenth century.'

He is suggesting that the Queen's own actions were less of a problem than people's expectations of what a queen should do – they were alarmed simply by her involvement in politics, something that was not expected of any woman.

The Jacobin Club

The Jacobin Club was one of hundreds of political clubs that had developed since 1789. It had emerged from the original meetings of a group of Breton deputies in 1789 and was given its name from the **Jacobin** convent in the Rue Saint-Honoré where they met. It charged high admission (12 livres) and membership fees (24 livres) which meant that its members were drawn from the wealthier sections of society. Crucially these men tended to be politically active, many were deputies, and in their debates they discussed the issues that arose in the National Assembly. Meeting four times a week it acted as a pressure group for first patriot and then radical (i.e. revolutionary) ideas. By June 1791 it had roughly 2400 members. Across France a network of Jacobin clubs developed in towns and cities (833 of them by June 1791) which communicated by letter with the central club in Paris. Together these became a powerful political force. Robespierre was to emerge as the leader of the Jacobins.

Following the attempted royal flight to Varennes, the political pace was set by the radicals in the Jacobin Club. A petition was drawn up by Danton and Brissot and others. This stated that the King had, in effect, abdicated and that he should not be replaced unless the majority of the nation agreed to it. This was a republican manifesto, advocating the end of the experiment with constitutional monarchy.

Its immediate result was that the Jacobin Club split. The majority of its members, including most of the National Assembly deputies, were constitutional monarchists and were glad to split from the more radical republican members. They left to set up a new pro-monarchy club known as the **Feuillants** because they met at the former monastery of the Feuillants. One of the few deputies left in the Jacobin Club was Robespierre. He persuaded its remaining members to withdraw their support for the petition but was too late. Members of the new Feuillants would not return to the Jacobin Club and the idea of preparing a petition was taken up by the more radical Cordeliers Club.

1. Make notes which explain: the Queen's attitudes to constitutional monarchy; how her reputation and attitude affected expectations that the system could work.

2. Now place Marie Antoinette on your continuum line, adding brief notes to justify this placement.

Jacobin was the name given to Dominican monks in Paris. When the Breton deputies began to hold their meetings in the Jacobins' former convent they were mockingly called Jacobins by their opponents in the National Assembly, suggesting they were some sort of monks.

Feuillants
Monks from Feuillant Abbey, a house of the Cistercian order of monks

1 Make notes to explain: the attitude of the Jacobins and Cordeliers Club to constitutional monarchy.

2 Place each of these groups on your continuum line, adding brief notes to justify its placement. You may want to revisit this when you find out what happened later.

1 Make notes to explain: the views of the Club Monarchique and the *émigrés*; the extent of their influence; why they increased fear of counter-revolution.

2 Place the Club Monarchique and the *émigrés* on your continuum line, adding brief notes to justify this placement.

Pillnitz Declaration
A joint declaration by Leopold II of Austria and Frederick-William II of Prussia in which they threatened a combined military intervention in French affairs on behalf of the French monarchy.

The Cordeliers Club

The Cordeliers Club originated in the Cordeliers district of Paris in May 1790 and was more radical than the Jacobins at this time (though some people belonged to both clubs). It had a much lower admission charge and monthly subscription so its membership was large. Many Parisians could afford to belong and, unlike the Jacobins, women members were allowed. The leadership tended to be middle class and notably included Danton and Desmoulins, Marat and Hébert. The Cordeliers saw their role as politically educating the common people, keeping an eye on the actions of the deputies, acting as bodyguards to protect popular leaders and as leaders of the democratic movement. They took their support from the people of Paris, the very people who the National Assembly deputies were anxious to exclude from the political process. So the Cordeliers had an interest in constitutional monarchy failing.

Following Louis' failed flight to Varennes and the subsequent split in the Jacobin Club, the Cordeliers organised a signing ceremony for Danton and Brissot's petition for a republic on the Champs de Mars on 17 July 1791. By the afternoon roughly 50,000 people were gathered and thousands had signed. However, two men found hiding under the platform on which was a table with the petition for people to sign, were accused of being spies and lynched. This gave Bailly, the mayor of Paris, the excuse to declare martial law and call out the National Guard. Under Lafayette, and in response to stone throwing from the crowd, the National Guard opened fire. Between 12 and 50 were killed and the rest scattered in what is known as the Massacre of the Champs de Mars. In its aftermath its leaders fled abroad (Danton), were arrested (Desmoulins) or went into hiding (Marat). The Cordeliers Club was shut down.

The Club Monarchique and the *émigrés*

On the political far right there were clubs such as the Club Monarchique, a counter-revolutionary group which emerged in 1790. At its height it had some 200 members. Among them were deputies of the National Assembly and men from the clergy, the nobility and the upper bourgeoisie. It sponsored counter-revolutionary propaganda, fostered links with the *émigrés* and used charity to build popular support in Paris. It encouraged the formation of similar clubs across France such as Amis du Roi. These worked for a return to the monarchy of the Ancien Régime.

The *émigrés* were nobles who had emigrated from France since the Revolution began including Louis' youngest brother, the Comte Artois, who had left in July 1789. He set up his court in Turin and plotted to overthrow the Revolution despite Louis asking him not to do so. Louis viewed their actions as jeopardising his negotiating position and increasing popular fears of counter-revolution. Following the failed flight to Varennes in 1791, their numbers were swelled by thousands more, including Louis' younger brother the Comte de Provence. Their activities, such as calling on foreign rulers for military help, increased fears of counter-revolution. The **Pillnitz Declaration** in August 1791 added to those fears.

The *sans-culottes*

The *sans-culottes* were the most radical political group. In the reorganisation of local government in 1790, Paris was divided into 48 sections and these became the power base of the *sans-culottes*. It was they who had stormed the Bastille and who forced the royal family to leave Versailles for Paris. But they did not seem to be benefiting from the Revolution. Many did not qualify to be voters ('active citizens') and their livelihoods were threatened by the high food prices resulting from the poor harvest of 1791. They responded with strikes and riots and pressed for the right to vote. Their radical demands for the Revolution to go further, put pressure on the process of trying to make constitutional monarchy work.

In 1791 the *sans-culottes* intervened directly in events again. Louis XVI was a devout man and his conscience was troubled by his acceptance of the Civil Constitution of the Clergy. This led him to hear Mass said by a refractory priest. News of this caused outrage. People felt they could not trust Louis and there were rumours he would try to escape the city. So in April when he tried to go to Saint Cloud a huge crowd blocked his carriage, a moment that was to have future significance since it led to Louis' decision to leave Paris secretly.

The Feuillants

The former Jacobins opposed to republicanism were known as the Feuillants. Some of its members had come from the Société de 1789, an elitist, constitutional monarchist pressure group founded in January 1790 as a direct response to the Jacobins. The Société de 1789 included Lafayette, Mirabeau and Sieyès amongst its membership and it tried to influence National Assembly deputies by persuasion at dinners.

By August 1791, following the Champs de Mars Massacre and the closure of the Cordeliers Club, the Jacobins were in disarray and newspapers were shut down. The Feuillants were the dominant group and they controlled the National Assembly because their arguments won over many non-Feuillant deputies. This enabled them to complete the new constitution spelling out how a constitutional monarchy would work.

The Constitution was formally signed by Louis on 13 September. The National Assembly met for the final time on 30 September to be replaced the next day by the new Legislative Assembly. But although it appeared that the Feuillants had secured the constitutional monarchy there was one significant problem. Back in May, at Robespierre's suggestion, the deputies had passed the self-denying decree. This meant that no National Assembly deputies could stand for the new Legislative Assembly. It meant that when the Legislative Assembly met, the men who had written the Constitution were not there to defend it.

> **1** Make notes to explain: why the *sans-culottes* were dissatisfied with the constitutional monarchy; which of their actions played a part in its downfall.
>
> **2** Place the *sans-culottes* on your continuum line, adding brief notes to justify its placement.

> **1** Make notes to explain: why the Feuillants were in control by August 1791; the main points of the new constitution; what the Feuillants failed to do to defend the new constitution.
>
> **2** Place the Feuillants on your continuum line, adding brief notes to justify its placement. Reconsider the place of the Jacobins in the light of Robespierre's self-denying ordinance.

New constitution

The King:

- appoints ministers, conducts foreign policy and is head of the armed forces
- has a civil list or funding from the state of 25 million livres per annum
- cannot block legislation but can veto it. This veto suspends legislation for between two and four years.

Legislative Assembly:

- is one body with 745 deputies to be elected every two years
- has control of all legislation, government finances and the armed forces
- can impeach ministers.

1 Make notes to explain: why the Jacobin deputies could take the lead in the Legislative Assembly; why Louis used his veto.

2 Place the Legislative Assembly Deputies on your continuum line, adding brief notes to justify the placement.

Legislative Assembly Deputies

Elections took place at the end of August so that on the 1 October the 745 new deputies of the Legislative Assembly could start work. All these deputies were well off, as expected from an election system which favoured the wealthy (see page 64). The deputies were almost entirely drawn from the bourgeoisie. There were few nobles, most having either emigrated or retired to live quietly on their country estates; and there were a few clergy.

The political position of the deputies was made clear by which club they joined: 136 joined the Jacobins and 264 joined the Feuillants. This seemed to give the Feuillants most power but they needed the support of the 345 unaligned deputies and many of these distrusted the King and his commitment to the constitution he had signed.

Because so many deputies distrusted the King, this allowed the Jacobin republican Brissot and his radical supporters to control the assembly debates. They led on the two most important issues, how to deal with the refractory clergy and the *émigrés*, both seen as counter-revolutionary threats. On 29 November the deputies passed a law that any refractory clergy who continued to refuse to swear the oath would be regarded as conspiring against the nation. Louis, a devout Catholic, could not possibly agree with this and vetoed it. He also vetoed a second law passed on the same day which demanded the return of the King's brothers and threatened to confiscate the property of any *émigré* who did not return. The deputies, who wanted a republic, had deliberately backed Louis into the position where they knew he would use his veto. This made Louis even more unpopular because he seemed to be deliberately obstructing the work of the Legislative Assembly.

The Feuillants had failed to achieved their aims and all agreed so had constitutional monarchy. The British ambassador, Earl Gower, wrote, 'The present constitution has no friends and cannot last.'

■ Concluding your enquiry

Look at your completed continuum.

1 Re-assess the place of each one in the light of your understanding of this whole period.

2 Who do you now see as being most to blame for the failure of constitutional monarchy? You could think about the following questions.

- Did the Feuillants such as Lafayette, do enough to ensure the success of constitutional monarchy?

- Were the radical deputies determined to prevent constitutional monarchy from succeeding by pushing the Civil Constitution of the Clergy and the oath of loyalty?

- Does the blame lie with Louis and Marie Antoinette for increasing distrust and fear of counter-revolution?

- How significant was Robespierre's self-denying decree?

When was the turning point?

An alternative enquiry into this period would be to consider which of these two events was the key turning point in the failure of constitutional monarchy:

■ 27 November 1790 when the National Assembly deputies demanded the oath of the clergy or 20 June 1791 Louis' flight to Varennes?

Whilst, as William Doyle writes, the oath did force the people of France to make a choice (were they for or against the Revolution?) I would argue that the key turning point was Louis' mistaken attempt to leave Paris, and in secrecy, because from then on his reign was doomed as both Furet and Tackett suggest below. What do you think?

   Look back at your notes and the overview on page 63 and then read what the four historians below have to say. Then decide.

The French Revolution had many turning points; but the oath of the clergy was, if not the greatest, unquestionably one of them. It was certainly the Constituent Assembly's most serious mistake. For the first time revolutionaries forced fellow citizens to choose; to declare themselves publicly for or against the new order.

(William Doyle, *The Oxford History of the French Revolution*, Second Edition (2002).)

But a full explanation of the origins of the Terror must also reflect on the impact of the attempted flight of the king. The dramatic effort of Louis XVI and his family to escape the capital and abandon the new government … set in motion an extraordinary chain of actions and reactions with profound effects on all elements of society and virtually every corner of the nation.

(Timothy Tackett *When the King Took Flight* (2003).)

Given the divisiveness engendered by the Civil Constitution of the Clergy and the Clerical Oath, some might point to November 1790 and the months that followed as a crucial turning point for revolutionary France. Certainly resentment over the legislation gave impetus to the counter-revolutionary movements that would plague France, particularly in the Vendée, for the rest of the decade. On the other hand, it seems likely that many devout Catholics would have come to oppose the Revolution as it grew more radical even had their priests not been required to swear an oath of loyalty.

(Paul Hanson, *Contesting the French Revolution* (2009).)

Louis XVI started to die on 21 June 1791. He was not yet a hostage, but he was already little more than a stake in the game. For his flight tore away the veil of that false constitutional monarchy and once more confronted the patriot party with the whole problem of the revolution's future.

(François Furet, *The French Revolution* (1988).)

73

The Revolution in the West Indies

In 1789 France had colonies in the West Indies. The main ones were the islands of Guadeloupe and Martinique; and most important of all Saint Domingue, the richest colony in the world. These colonies produced sugar, coffee and indigo and the trade in these was very profitable for both the colonists and for merchants back in the Atlantic ports of Bordeaux and Nantes. Associated with this was the equally profitable slave trade with West Africa. Income from these trades contributed significantly to the prosperity of France.

French colonies in the Caribbean *c.*1789

In Saint Domingue 40,000 white colonists controlled 500,000 black slaves. Needless to say these white colonists resisted any move to abolish slavery by the Society of the Friends of Blacks back in Paris, whose founding members in 1788 included Brissot, Lafayette and Mirabeau. On Saint Domingue there were also 30,000 mulattoes *(gens de couleur)* who were free people of African descent. They worked as overseers and some were property owners and even slave owners themselves. In 1789 these men sent a delegation to Paris, led by Vincent Ogé, to seek equal rights for *gens de couleur*. In the debates that followed some feared this would set a precedent and lead to the abolition of slavery altogether whilst others saw freedom for blacks as consistent with the ideals of the Revolution. The colonists' pressure group, the Club de l'Hotel de Massiac, won the argument and on 8 March 1790 the National Assembly voted to exclude the colonies from both the Declaration of Rights and the Constitution.

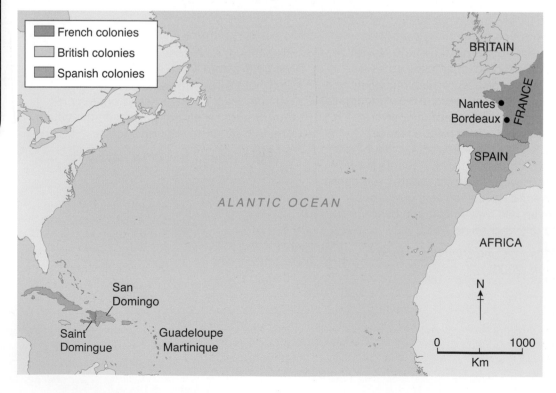

Ogé returned to Saint Domingue and campaigned in the elections. White colonists were appalled and tried to stop him which provoked a rebellion that failed. In 1791 Ogé himself was **broken on the wheel**. However, these disturbances triggered a wider slave rebellion that in August 1791 devastated the colony, with over 1000 white colonists killed, 200 sugar and 1200 coffee plantations destroyed. Over 15,000 black slaves escaped. To avoid similar rebellions the colonists in Martinique and Guadalupe granted reforms. In France, in January and February 1792 the effects of the rebellion were felt in the form of shortages of sugar and coffee and prices that tripled. This led to protests and riots in Paris which helped those planning to overthrow the monarchy.

Being **broken on the wheel** was when the criminal was tied to a wheel and then each of their limbs broken by the executioner using an iron bar. Sometimes the body would be left on display still tied to the wheel and mounted on the top of a post. Ogé's agonising death was a stark reminder to the revolutionaries back in France of the fate that awaited them if the Revolution failed.

Meanwhile, several leading Girondins (see page 79) joined the Society of the Friends of the Blacks and in April 1792 equal rights were given to all *gens de couleur*. However, this did not affect slavery and even amid all the disruption of 1792, 10,000 new African slaves were brought to Saint Domingue. In 1793, following the trial and execution of Louis, some colonists in the Saint Domingue considered an offer to become part of the British Empire. The British, who were now at war with France, sent troops to Saint Domingue and the Spanish invaded from their side of the island and promised freedom to any slaves who fought for them. This led to a complex mix of invasion and civil war. In an attempt to gain the support of the black population, the local French republican leadership abolished slavery, something that the National Convention back in Paris endorsed with a decree on 4 February 1794. In the short term this was very successful. Many blacks changed sides and, led by Toussaint L'Ouverture, drove out the Spanish. However, they then went on to kill any white colonists who had welcomed those invaders. By 1798 the last British troops had left and whilst still loyal to France, L'Ouverture was in control. Meanwhile, back in France the disruption to the sugar trade led to price rises in Paris, and this in turn aided the Montagnards (see page 79) in their political struggle with the Girondins. During this whole period, France's income from the colony was seriously damaged which was a significant economic blow.

That is how the situation remained until Napoleon came to power after the Coup of Brumaire in 1799. He sent an expeditionary force of 20,000 men to regain control of the colony. L'Ouverture was kidnapped and sent to France where he died in prison. But Napoleon's re-establishment of slavery in May 1802 led the former slaves and their allies, under the leadership of Jean-Jacques Dessalines, to keep fighting for their freedom and independence. A mixture of military successes and the death of so many French soldiers from yellow fever resulted in their eventual success. On the 1 January 1804 the new nation of **Haiti** came into existence. Estimates of the casualty figures for these conflicts suggest that as many as 100,000 blacks, 24,000 colonists and 50,000 French soldiers died.

Just as in France this revolution cost many lives but, unlike in France, the gains of this revolution were not immediately reversed. **Haiti** remains an independent country today although it is the poorest in the Americas.

Revolutionary leaders

Two of the leading revolutionaries were Georges Danton and Maximilien Robespierre but they were very different people.

Georges Jacques Danton (1759–94)

Danton was born on 26 October 1759, the fifth child of a petty bourgeois family. As a child he sustained facial injuries in an attack by a bull and he was also left scarred by smallpox. These, together with his great size, made him an intimidating figure. Added to this were his skills as an orator, honed in his legal practice before he entered politics.

Danton came to political prominence in the Cordeliers district and club in 1789, and later in the Jacobin Club where his speeches were legendary. He was one of the organisers of the event that led to the Massacre of the Champs de Mars in July 1791 (see page 71). Danton then went to England to avoid possible arrest but returned in September and in November was elected deputy *procureur* of Paris. From this important post he increased his power base in the city.

He was seen as the revolutionary who spoke for the *sans-culottes*. Therefore, he was a key figure, possibly the leader, in the final overthrow of the monarchy in August 1792. Immediately afterwards Danton was appointed Minister of Justice in the provisional government that controlled France until October. In that time he did not prevent the September Massacres but did crucially rally support for the war effort.

He was elected to the National Convention in 1792 where he sat in **'the Mountain'**. He came under attack from the Girondins who hated him for his complicity in the September Massacres (see page 86), for his corruption and for his links with General Dumouriez, who eventually defected to the Austrians. On the charges of corruption there is no doubt that Danton made money during the Revolution which he used to buy land. He voted for the death of Louis XVI and was instrumental in the setting up of the apparatus of the Terror, that is the Revolutionary Tribunal and the Committee of Public Safety of which he was one of the original nine members. He said, '… let us be terrible, to dispense the people from the need to be terrible themselves'. He was frequently sent on missions to the front of the Revolutionary Wars (see page 80) to bolster and support the morale of the generals and their troops.

Following illness and a spell at home, he returned to Paris and campaigned to end the Terror. He lost the resulting power struggle with Robespierre and was arrested, tried and executed. His last words to the executioner were: 'Don't forget to show my head to the people. It's well worth seeing.'

△ Danton, graphite sketch *c*. 1793 by Jacques-Louis David.

the Mountain (*montagne* in French)
This was the nickname for the benches high up on the left in the National Convention where the Jacobin deputies sat, hence their other name, the Montagnards

---

Verdicts on Danton

- Carlyle called Danton the 'Titan of the Revolution'.
- Another famous revolutionary, Lenin, admiringly described Danton as 'the greatest master of revolutionary tactics yet known'. He was referring to how Danton led the planning of the Insurrectionist Committee which successfully overthrew the monarchy by the attack on the Tuileries, 10 August 1792.
- David Lawday titled his 2009 biography *Danton: Gentle Giant of Terror*.

Maximilien Robespierre (1758–94)

Maximilien Robespierre was born in Arras, the son of a lawyer. Following the early death of his mother and the absence of his father he was brought up by his grandfather and aunts. He was educated as a scholarship boy at the College Louis-le-Grand in Paris where he first met and became friends with Camille Desmoulins. Here Robespierre was influenced by the ideals of the Ancient Roman Republic and most importantly by the ideas of Rousseau, especially those written in his *Social Contract* (see page 26). Following his education and subsequent legal training he returned to Arras to practise as a lawyer.

Robespierre first came to national attention in 1789 when he was elected as a deputy to the Estates-General. There he became well known for his Jacobin views, his belief in democracy and his opposition to both capital punishment and slavery. Of him Mirabeau said: 'That young man will go far because he believes everything he says.' Robespierre did indeed rise to prominence in the Jacobin Club and in August 1792 was elected to the National Convention. Here, he became a leader of the Montagnard faction opposed to the Girondins (see page 61). Unlike Danton, he gained a reputation as an incorruptible politician. He sought neither political office nor wealth. In 1792 he was living simply, lodging with the cabinet maker Maurice Duplay and his family in Rue Saint Honoré, conveniently close to the Jacobin Club and the meeting place of the National Convention.

When the Committee of Public Safety was first elected he declined to be a member but in July 1793 he joined the Committee and became its key member. To many people he then became the driving force behind the Terror which lasted from the middle of 1793 to July 1794 when Robespierre was arrested and executed. He justified the thousands of deaths in the Terror as being necessary to defend the Revolution against counter-revolutionary forces but his reputation has been much debated.

△ *Robespierre*, sketch by Jacques-Louis David. David also made some notes on the sketch. 'Eyes green, complexion pale, green striped nankeen jacket, blue waistcoat with blue stripes, white cravat striped with red.'

Verdicts on Robespierre

- Lord Acton (1910) described Robespierre as 'the most hateful character in the forefront of human history since Machiavelli reduced to a code the wickedness of public men.'
- James M Thompson (1939) wrote: 'so long as its [the French Revolution] leaders are sanely judged, with due allowance for the terrible difficulties of their task; so long will Robespierre, who lived and died for the Revolution, remain one of the great figures of history.'
- Ruth Scurr titled her 2006 biography *Fatal Purity: Robespierre and the French Revolution*.

For Marisa Linton's verdict on Robespierre, go to page 112.

7 Why did violence explode in August and September 1792?

> … I saw a woman appear, pale as her underclothing, held up by a counter clerk. They said to her in a harsh voice: 'Cry out "Long live the nation!"' 'No! no!' she said. They made her climb onto a heap of corpses. One of the murderers seized the counter clerk and took him away. 'Ah!' cried the unfortunate woman, 'don't hurt him!' They told her again to cry out 'Long live the nation!' she refused disdainfully. Then a killer seized her, tore off her dress and opened her belly. She fell and was finished off by the others. Never had such horror offered itself to my imagination. I tried to flee, my legs failed. I fainted. When I came to my senses I saw the bloody head. I was told that it had been washed, its hair curled, and that it had been put on the end of a pike and carried under the windows of *the Temple*. Pointless cruelty! …

the Temple
This was where the Princess de Lamballe's great friend, Marie Antoinette, was imprisoned

These words, written by an eye-witness, the novelist Restif de la Bretonne, describe the death of the Princess de Lamballe, close friend of Marie Antoinette. This was one moment, one death in the explosion of violence that shook Paris in August and September 1792, culminating in the September Massacres in which many hundreds of people suspected of counter-revolutionary activities were executed.

Tension had been building for more than a year, ever since Louis' failed flight to Varennes (June 1791) had destroyed his credibility as King in the eyes of many of his subjects. From that moment, some at least had begun to think of a future for France without a king, of France as a republic. However, there was no instant change. Louis remained King in name during the rest of 1791 and as 1792 unfolded, but nobody, of course, knew what lay ahead for him and the people of France.

Much of the growing tension was linked to wars with Austria and Prussia. These wars were a threat to the revolutionaries because French defeat might well see Austria and Prussia restore Louis as King with full powers and consequently the destruction of the Revolution. Mixed inextricably with these anxieties over how the wars might develop, was fear of counter-revolutionaries plotting within France, especially amongst and surrounding the royal family. Thus the revolutionaries felt under threat both from within and from outside France but were determined to defeat their enemies and safeguard the revolution.

The atmosphere of summer 1792 is wonderfully captured in the words of *La Marseillaise*, one of the most stirring national anthems. Nowadays we hear it most often at sports fixtures but it was composed by Rouget de l'Isle in 1792, at a moment of deep crisis for the Revolution, as the war song of the French army of the Rhine. The *fédérés* (the regional National Guard) of Marseilles sang it as they marched into Paris, summoned to protect the city from the Prussian army whose commander had threatened to destroy Paris if Louis was harmed. So popular was *La Marseillaise* that it was adopted as the anthem of the Republic on 14 July 1795.

Examine the words of *La Marseillaise* closely and you can feel the fear and resistance to the twin threats from counter-revolutionaries ('traitors and conjured kings') and foreign armies ('ferocious soldiers'). But above all, *La Marseillaise* is a call to arms, appealing to the 'citizens' of France to defend the Revolution.

That word 'citizens' tells us a great deal about how ideas had changed. With the experiment of constitutional monarchy dead or dying, the revolutionaries no longer saw themselves as 'subjects' of the king ('the old slavery' in *La Marseillaise*) but as 'citizens'. Now everyone should be free and equal. Hence the soldiers of the foreign armies, subjects of kings, are viewed as 'slaves' and the threat facing the citizens of France is that if absolute monarchy is restored then the French people will become slaves again. Given this fear, the explosion of violence in Paris in the summer of 1792 is far from surprising.

La Marseillaise

Arise, children of the Fatherland,

The day of glory has arrived!

Against us of tyranny

The bloody banner is raised, (repeat)

Do you hear, in the countryside,

The roar of those ferocious soldiers?

They're coming right into our arms

To cut the throats of our sons and women!

To arms, citizens,

Form your battalions,

Let's march, let's march!

That an impure blood

Waters our furrows!

What does this horde of slaves,

Of traitors and conjured kings want?

For whom are these vile chains,

These long-prepared irons? (repeat)

Frenchmen, for us, ah! What outrage

What fury it must arouse!

It is us they dare plan

To return to the old slavery!

■ **Enquiry Focus:** Why did violence explode in August and September 1792?

The mind map below shows the main factors behind this explosion of violence. Your task is to collect evidence showing the impact of these factors, to consider how they may be connected and to decide which of them were most significant. This is a good activity to do in collaboration with another person.

1 After each section of text, answer the questions in the blue boxes.

2 Annotate your own version of this mind map with brief examples of how each factor helped increase the possibility of violence or provoked actual violence. The developing map will therefore give you an overview of the impact of the factors.

The Revolutionary War – threats from other nations

Fear of counter-revolution and activities of the royal family

Why did the revolution become more violent?

Rivalries amongst revolutionaries

Deteriorating living conditions

March	War with Austria. Military defeats led to fear of the defeat of the Revolution.
June	Prussia declared war on France.
	Sans-culottes occupied the Tuileries Palace, making Louis wear a red cap of liberty.
	Fédérés arrived in Paris singing *La Marseillaise*.
August	Prussia issued the Brunswick manifesto, threatening the destruction of Paris if Louis was harmed. News reached Paris that the Prussian army was approaching.
	The monarchy was overthrown when *sans-culottes* attacked the Tuileries Palace, leading to many deaths. Louis was imprisoned.
September	The September Massacres in Paris of many hundreds of people believed to be counter-revolutionaries.
	Victories by French forces ended fears of defeat by foreign armies.
	France was declared a republic.
December	Louis was put on trial for crimes against the French people.

War and the build-up of tension August 1791 to May 1792

As the Revolution progressed, Austria, Britain, Prussia and Russia watched carefully. A weakened, distracted France was less of a threat to them but, on the other hand, they feared that any assault on a monarch was threatening to all other monarchies.

In August 1791 Austria and Prussia issued the Pillnitz Declaration which threatened military intervention in support of Louis. Although they did nothing, the threat and the presence of *émigré* troops under the Comte d'Artois, Louis' brother, in Coblenz (on France's north eastern frontier), made the revolutionaries even more suspicious of the royal family's attitudes and increased their fear of counter-revolution and invasion. They were right to be suspicious. In December, at the urging of the National Assembly deputies, Louis publicly demanded that the Elector of **Trier** disperse the *émigré* troops at Coblenz, yet at the same time Louis secretly asked the Elector not to do this.

Within France there were different views on the desirability of war against Austria. Louis was in favour, believing he would benefit, whatever the result. If a war went well he, as commander-in-chief, might recover his powers and if it went badly the Austrian victors would restore his old powers. Marie Antoinette also believed that Louis would benefit from France being defeated. In a letter in December 1791 she wrote, 'I do believe we are about to declare war … The imbeciles! They cannot see that this will serve us well, for … if we begin it, all the Powers will become involved.' She was expecting, looking forward to, defeat. The generals, Lafayette and Dumouriez, also believed a short, successful war would strengthen the authority of the King and increase their own prestige and influence.

Trier and Mainz were small states on the Rhine where the *émigrés* were based. Their hereditary rulers had been known as Electors since the Middle Ages when the Holy Roman Emperor was elected by the rulers of German states. (See the map on page 81.)

On the other side of the political divide the republican Brissot and other Girondins also argued for war but for a very different reason. They believed war would force Louis to reveal his true position, for or against the Revolution, and would bring other traitors out into the open. They claimed that counter-revolutionaries, a shadowy **Austrian Committee**, were plotting around Marie Antoinette. Brissot also wanted to spread the Revolution beyond France, believing the people of other nations would fight alongside the invading French armies to overthrow their own rulers.

In contrast, Robespierre opposed the war believing generals like Lafayette threatened the Revolution and had ambitions of their own. Robespierre also argued that people of other countries would not rise up and fight alongside the French invaders. He famously commented: 'No one loves armed missionaries.'

The Feuillants, such as Barnave, were also against war believing peace gave a better chance of preserving the gains of the Revolution, which for them had gone far enough. But their influence was destroyed when Louis replaced them as ministers with Brissot and his Girondins. The pro-war groups had won the argument. On 20 April 1792 Louis announced that France was at war with Austria. Only 7 out of 745 deputies voted against war.

Rumours of an **Austrian Committee** were developed in the popular press by writers like Desmoulins from 1790 onwards. It was supposed to meet in the Tuileries under the direction of Marie Antoinette with the intention of plotting with foreign countries, especially Austria, against the Revolution.

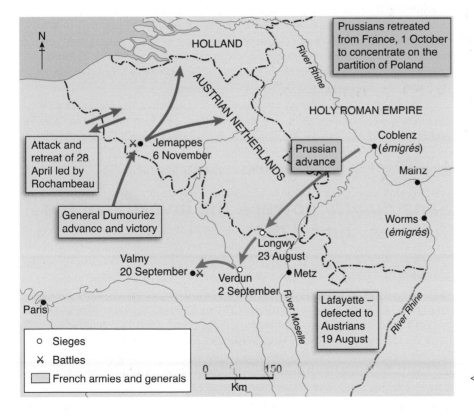

◁ The Revolutionary War in 1792.

The hoped-for successful war against Austria never materialised. Half the officers of the French army had become *émigrés* and the soldiers were a mixture of demoralised regulars and untried volunteers. Advancing into the Austrian Netherlands they were not welcomed by the population but instead (as Robespierre had predicted) met serious opposition. Soon they were in full retreat, murdering one of their generals on the way. Desertion rates in the cavalry doubled and the French generals called for peace talks.

Back in Paris the Girondins, anxious to turn blame away from themselves, accused the generals, the King and the Austrian Committee of betraying France. There was some truth to this last point, although they did not know it, as Marie Antoinette had secretly passed on the French military plans to her Austrian contacts. The language the Girondins used was inflammatory. One Girondin deputy, Elie Guadet, said: 'Let us mark out a place for traitors and let that place be a scaffold.' Defeat had heightened the likelihood of violence.

In an atmosphere of near panic, a number of measures were passed by the Legislative Assembly in May and June which show the extent of fear of counter-revolution. All foreigners in Paris were placed under surveillance. Refractory priests were to be deported. Louis vetoed this but he did agree to his personal bodyguard of 1800 men being disbanded. All regular troops stationed in and around Paris were sent to the front so they could not be used in a royalist military take-over. To replace them it was planned to set up a camp of *fédérés*, provincial National Guards, just outside Paris. Louis vetoed this too but *fédérés* arrived in Paris anyway for the annual 14 July parade. Meanwhile Louis changed ministers again, dismissing the Girondins who had criticised him and replacing them with Feuillants.

In addition Lafayette denounced the Girondins and visited Paris to try to persuade the National Guard to support the King and close the Jacobin Club. He was shunned by all sides as Marie Antoinette hated him and the deputies of the Legislative Assembly feared he planned a military dictatorship. He returned, disappointed, having only fuelled fears of counter-revolution.

Sans-culotte power – the invasion of the Tuileries, June 1792

The *sans-culottes* had first made their presence felt in the Revolution in the *journées* of 1789. By 1792 the 48 Sections of Paris were becoming centres of militancy dominated by the *sans-culottes*. Each section was run by its own officials and committees. From 1793 this included the powerful **Surveillance or Watch Committees**. Each section sent two representatives to sit on the Paris Commune, the Municipal (or City) Government of Paris.

The *sans-culottes* wanted more extreme measures than the deputies in the Legislative Assembly, such as price controls on food and the right to vote to benefit the lower classes. The value of the livre and *assignats* had fallen significantly, pushing up the price of food and there were shortages of sugar (which tripled in price) after the slave rebellion and subsequent civil war in Saint Domingue (see pages 74–75). These developments triggered riots in Paris in January and February 1792 and all served to make the *sans-culottes* more militant. Other events of 1792 (particularly the war propaganda of the Girondins, the military defeats, Louis' use of his veto and dismissal of his Girondin ministers, and Lafayette's call for the

Jacobin Club to be shut down) all served to increase the militancy of the *sans-culottes* still further.

On 20 June all these frustrations came to a head. Thousands of *sans-culottes* occupied the Tuileries and forced Louis to wear a red cap of liberty. He behaved with great courage on the day, resisted their demands to reinstate the Girondin ministers and withdraw his veto, and eventually the demonstrators were peacefully persuaded to disperse. There had been no violence as yet but tension was growing ever higher.

△ A section from *A Sans-culotte with His Pike, a Carter, a Market Porter, a Cobbler and a Carpenter*, a Giclee print by the Le Sueur Brothers.

Sans-culottes — a criminal rabble or respectable workers?

Not all historians attach the same importance or give the same attention to the *sans-culottes*. One who did was the British Marxist historian George Rudé, an advocate of 'history from below' (see page 53). In *The Crowd in the French Revolution* (1959), he analysed the records of 120 of the 300 Parisians killed in the attack on the Tuileries whose occupations are known.

'Of this number as many as 95 are drawn from 50 of the petty trades and crafts of the capital either as shopkeepers, small traders and manufacturers, master craftsmen, artisans, or journeymen. There are only two bourgeois and three that may be termed professional men among them: an architect, a surgeon, and a drawing master. The rest are clerks (20), musicians (2), domestic servants (9), port workers, labourers, and carters (7), and glass workers (2) ... there are surprisingly many wage-earners among them: 33 journeymen and 18 other workers. Yet, even so, they form considerably less than half the total. In all then, they are typical *sans-culottes*, with a sprinkling of more or less prosperous citizens ...'

Rudé, as a Marxist historian, was in part responding to historians on the political right who characterised the *sans-culottes* as a mob or rabble (*la canaille*), vagrants, beggars and common criminals. Rudé argued they were respectable workers and artisans of modest means but he also believed they were a definable social group. More recently revisionist historians such as Richard Andrews see the *sans-culottes* not as a social class but as a political grouping, a subtle but important difference.

The onrush of violence, August 1792

In July the deputies declared a state of national emergency after Prussia had joined the war against France. In a climate of increasing fear, Robespierre called for the abolition of the monarchy. Provincial National Guards (*fédérés*) began to arrive in Paris, joining increased calls for the end of the monarchy, and a law of 30 July allowed '**passive citizens**' to join the National Guard, a clear boost to *sans-culotte* power. An **Insurrectionist Committee** began to meet secretly in Paris. Its very secrecy means it is difficult to know exactly what was said or who attended but it certainly involved Danton and many *sans-culottes*. Also possibly involved were Marat, whose journal *L'Ami du peuple* continually called for democracy and violence, and Robespierre, who led the Jacobins and was very influential with the *fédérés*. But whatever was said and whoever was involved it was instrumental in the *journée* of 10 August which overthrew the monarchy.

passive citizens
Those men over 25 who, under the 1791 constitution, had full civic rights but did not have the right to vote because they did not pay tax equivalent to 3 days' wages

Central to the outbreak of violence was the issue of the Brunswick Manifesto by the Duke of Brunswick in August 1792. Written by an *émigré*, the manifesto set out Prussia's purpose which was to enter (though not conquer) France, restore the freedom of Louis XVI, make the city of Paris responsible for Louis' safety and threatened to inflict 'an exemplary vengeance' on the city and its citizens if the Tuileries were attacked and the royal family harmed.

News of the manifesto's contents inflamed public opinion against Louis even more. For those who were plotting an attack on the Tuileries it showed that they could not afford to fail and the final, decisive *journée* of 10 August 1792 overthrew the monarchy. On the previous night of the 9 August there was an atmosphere of fear and uncertainty in the Tuileries Palace. No one slept. There had been rumours in Paris of an organised attack on the Tuileries to overthrow the monarchy and during the night alarm bells rang all over the city. Paris itself was like an armed camp, filled with the *fédérés* from the provinces who had stopped on their way to the war front, including those recently arrived from Marseilles. The palace itself was defended by a garrison of 2000 National Guards, 800 Swiss Guards and between 100 and 200 courtiers and former officers who had come to protect the King, the 'knights of the dagger' (*chevaliers du poignard*) as they were described. At 6.00a.m. the garrison commander, the Marquis de Mandat, was summoned to the Hotel de Ville where he found Danton in control. Mandat was arrested and then murdered, the first of many to die that day.

Thousands of men, (*sans-culottes*, *fédérés* and National Guards) were massed to attack. This is how Madame de Tourzel, governess of the royal children who was in the Tuileries that day, describes what happened next in her memoires:

> About 7a.m. it was announced that the inhabitants of the faubourgs and the Marseillais were advancing against the chateau …

She goes on to describe the scene in the King's bedchamber when Roederer, who was in charge of the National Guard spoke to Louis. It was already apparent from events earlier that morning that the members of the National Guard who were supposed to be defending the palace, would go over to the side of the attackers.

> 'Sire the danger is imminent; the authorities have no force at their disposal and defence is impossible. Your Majesty and your family, as well as everybody in the chateau are in greatest danger; to prevent bloodshed there is no other resource than to repair to the assembly'. The Queen, who was standing by the King, remarked that it was impossible to abandon all the brave men who had come to the chateau solely to defend the King. 'If you oppose this step,' said Roederer to her in a severe voice, 'you will be responsible, Madame for the lives of the King and your children.' The poor unhappy Queen was silent and experienced such a revulsion of feeling that her face and neck became suffused with colour. She was distressed beyond measure to see the King listen to the advice of a man as justifiably suspect …

But listen Louis did and at about 8.00a.m. he agreed to take his family, including Madame de Tourzel, to seek refuge with the Legislative Assembly.

The story is next taken up by a National Guardsman writing a letter to a friend in Rennes the next day.

Hardly was the King safe than the noise of cannon fire increased. The Breton *fédérés* beat a tattoo. Some officers suggested retreat to the commander of the Swiss guards. But he seemed prepared and soon, by a clever tactic, captured the artillery which the national guard held in the courtyard. These guns, now turned on the people, fire and strike them down. But soon the conflict is intensified everywhere. The Swiss, surrounded, overpowered, stricken, then run out of ammunition. They plead for mercy, but it is impossible to calm the people, furious at Helvetian treachery.

The Swiss are cut to pieces. Some were killed in the state-rooms, others in the garden. Many died on the Champs-Elysées. Heavens! That liberty should cost Frenchmen blood and tears! How many victims there were among both the people and the national guard! The total number of dead could run to 2000. All the Swiss who had been taken prisoner were escorted to the Place de Grève. There they had their brains blown out. They were traitors sacrificed to vengeance. What vengeance! I shivered to the roots of my being. At least 47 heads were cut off. The Grève was littered with corpses, and heads were paraded on the ends of several pikes. The first heads to be severed were those of seven *chevaliers du poignard*, slain at 8 o'clock in the morning on the Place Vendôme. Many Marseillais perished in the *journée* of 10 August.

▽ *The Taking of the Tuileries Palace (Prise du palais des Tuileries)*, painted in 1793 by Jean Duplessis-Bertaux.

1 Make notes using this question as a guide: what part did each of the following play in the outbreak of violence in August:
- changing living standards
- the impact of war
- the actions of Louis and Lafayette?

2 What examples of greater violence are there in this period? How great was the increase in violence?

3 Add summary examples to your mind map of how some factors increased the possibility of violence.

Some historians call the period between the 17 August and the 6 September 1792 the **First Terror**.

By mid-day it was all over, the bloodiest day of the Revolution so far. The Insurrectionist Commune was now in control of Paris. The deputies of the Legislative Assembly were forced to hand over Louis and he was imprisoned. The deputies were also forced to agree to a new election, by universal male suffrage, of a National Convention that was to draw up a new democratic constitution for the Republic. The monarchy was over.

The First Terror and the September Massacres

In the aftermath of the taking of the Tuileries, Louis and his family were imprisoned by the Insurrectionist Commune. Power was now shared between the deputies of the Legislative Assembly, the Insurrectionist Commune who controlled Paris and a new body created by them both, the Provisional Executive Council which was dominated by Danton. These three groups held power until September 1792 when the new National Convention was put in place. In another sign of changing times, an Extraordinary Tribunal was set up on the 17 August to try those who had 'committed counter-revolutionary offences'. In this **First Terror**, a few people were found guilty and guillotined for the crime of being a royalist.

Meanwhile the revolutionary war continued. On 19 August the Prussian army invaded France and on the same day, when his own army refused to march on Paris to help him overthrow Brissot and his supporters (see page 83), Lafayette defected to the Austrians. When the frontier fortress of Longwy was easily captured it seemed that the Prussians would capture Paris within weeks. In response the Insurrectionist Commune ordered the arrest of all suspected counter-revolutionaries. Hundreds were imprisoned but rumours spread that these counter-revolutionaries would break out of the prisons, massacre the people and surrender the city to the advancing Prussians. Marat and other extremists called for them to be killed.

The killing known as the September Massacres started after the fortress of Verdun fell on 1 September, leaving Paris unprotected from the Prussian army. Next day crowds surrounded a tumbrel (wagon) of prisoners on its way to the Abbaye prison and murdered them on the spot. Groups of *sans-culottes* then invaded other prisons and set up impromptu courts. Prisoners were dragged from their cells, tried, then hacked or beaten to death in the prison courtyards. Over five days between 1100 and 1300 prisoners out of the 2600 held in Paris prisons were murdered. Amongst them were 200 refractory priests, what was left of the Swiss guards and many known royalists; but the rest were ordinary criminals who were simply suspected of being in the pay of the counter-revolutionaries. Whilst the massacres were taking place, the Paris Commune did nothing to stop them and afterwards even voted to pay the murderers for their work. The killings shocked Paris, France and the rest of Europe. None of the revolutionary leaders came out to openly condemn the killings but they did accuse each other of responsibility or complicity. Danton, for example, as Minister of Justice was blamed for doing nothing, as was Roland who was Minister of the Interior.

■ **Concluding your enquiry**

1 Make notes using these questions as a guide:
   - How did Lafayette and events in the war contribute to increased fear of counter-revolution?
   - What examples are there in this period of greater violence?
   - How great was the increase in violence?

2 Add summary examples to your mind map of how some factors increased the possibility of violence.

3 Read pages 88–89. How do the views presented there challenge the enquiry question in this chapter in their analysis of the role of violence in the Revolution?

4 Review your completed mind map. Which factors seem most significant in the explosion of violence in August and September? What connections can you see between the various factors?

5 Write a short summary explaining why the Revolution became so violent. Use your mind map to provide structure.

Postscript – the execution of the King

Two weeks after the September Massacres, on 20 September 1792, the 749 new deputies of the National Convention met for the first time. They were mostly lawyers, professional men and property owners and for the first time there were a few artisans. Amongst the deputies there was a clear division. Seated on the high benches on the left of the chair were those who came to be known as Montagnards, from 'the Mountain' where they sat. Opposing them were those on the right who came to be known as Girondins. Both groups had been members of the Jacobin Club. In between sat the main group of uncommitted deputies. Both Girondins and Montagnards were committed revolutionaries and republicans who wanted a fairer and more humane France. So how might they be distinguished from one another?

- The Girondins were marginally more moderate. They were pro war and hostile towards the *sans-culottes*.

- The Montagnards wanted the King punished and were prepared to accept *sans-culotte* support.

- The Girondins also accused the Montagnards of wanting to impose a political dictatorship and of being responsible for the September Massacres.

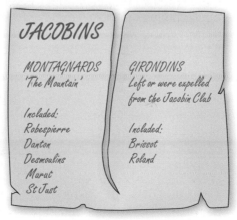

◁ The opposing revolutionary factions who once made up the Jacobin Club.

The question of the now deposed King had to be addressed. The deputies disagreed on what to do with Louis. The Girondins wanted a trial and to hold Louis as a hostage for possible future use. The Montagnards viewed him as already guilty and wanted him punished without trial. The Girondins won the argument and persuaded the deputies to agree to put Louis on trial for over 30 crimes against the French people.

The verdict was never in any doubt, especially after the discovery of the *armoire de fer*, an iron wall safe in the Tuileries which contained correspondence between Louis and the Austrians. Even so the sentence remained in doubt. Robespierre and the Montagnards argued for the death penalty whilst the Girondins wanted the sentence to be subject to a referendum of the people. They believed the people of the provinces, unlike the people of Paris, would not want Louis' death. But their efforts failed. Louis was found guilty and was then sentenced to death. On 21 January 1793 the sentence was carried out.

The fate of Marie Antoinette

After the King's execution the Queen acquired her last nickname, 'Widow **Capet**'. Finally, in 1793 she was separated from her children, transferred to the Conciergerie prison and then subjected to a show trial. She was accused of making secret agreements with foreign powers and sending them money, of conspiring against the French state and even of sexually abusing her own son. A guilty verdict was never in doubt. On Wednesday 16 October 1793 she was guillotined, ironically by the son of Louis' executioner.

After the storming of the Tuileries and being deposed as King, Louis was known as Louis **Capet**.

Was violence always central to the Revolution?

Not all historians would see the violence of September 1792 as a sudden explosion. Some on the political right have argued that violence was inherent in the Revolution from the very beginning. This viewpoint was popular during the Vichy years but was then discredited, along with that government. It was revived in the 1980s by French historian François Furet and it is the view advanced by Simon Schama in *Citizens* (1989).

> ... the carnage of the tenth of August was not an incidental moment in the history of the Revolution. It was, in fact, its logical consummation. From 1789 onwards, perhaps even before that, it had been the willingness of politicians to exploit either the threat or fact of violence that had given them the power to challenge constituted authority. Bloodshed was not the unfortunate by-product of revolution, it was the source of its energy. The verses of the Marseillaise and the great speeches of the Girondins had spoken of *patrie* in the absolute poetry of life and death.

Later in *Citizens*, Schama restates his claim:

> However much the historian, in a year of celebration, may be tempted to see that violence as an unpleasant 'aspect' of the revolution which ought not to distract from its accomplishments, it would be jejune to do so. From the very beginning – from the summer of 1789 – violence was the motor of the Revolution.

However there are many historians who take a different view seeing the Revolution as being blown off course by the violence. Their argument is that the Revolution came under attack from enemies both within and outside France and that violence was an unfortunate but necessary response. That places the blame not just on the revolutionaries but also on the counter-revolutionaries. I agree with those historians who view the revolutionary violence as a response to the threat or actual violence of the counter-revolutionaries. Before the attack on the Bastille the crowds were attacked by Louis' cavalry in the Tuileries gardens, and that attack itself only turned violent when the garrison fired on the crowd. And the same was true on 10 August.

From his research into the crowd in the 1789 protests the historian Micah Alpaugh (2009) claims that:

> … Revolutionary protesters did not necessarily set out to commit physical violence in the **Réveillon** riots, the taking of the Bastille or the October Days, and that their actions during the early phases of these events most closely corresponded to already developing, predominantly non-violent practices. The escalation of the *journées* into bloody insurrections was compelled to a substantial degree by attempted state repression, causing protesters to turn to more extreme tactics.

> **Réveillon** was a wealthy, wallpaper manufacturer whose Paris factory employed 300 workers. In April 1789 he was reported to have made comments about cutting wages which sparked off riots. During these riots his house and factory were destroyed but there was no loss of life until the troops brought in to restore order opened fire leaving 25 dead and others wounded.

The 'Machinery of Terror'

The phrase, the 'machinery of terror' is used by the historian Hugh Gough in his book *The Terror in the French Revolution* to refer to 'The Committee of Public Safety, the revolutionary tribunal, representatives on mission, watch committees and the law of 19 March ...', in other words, a series of government bodies and laws voted through by the deputies in the National Convention in March and early April 1793.

Therefore, in talking about terror here we do not mean terrorists trying to attack a state or states but the way in which a state tries to control its own population through fear. The same phrase 'machinery of terror' is also used by historians of the Soviet Union under Stalin and of Nazi Germany under Hitler. In the more recent past you can find references to the 'machinery of terror' in places such as Zimbabwe, Sri Lanka, and the Dominican Republic.

△ Cogs in the Machinery of Terror.

Committee of General Security (CGS)

At the beginning of 1793 one committee that became a vital component of the Machinery of Terror was already in existence. This was the Committee of General Security. It had developed out of an earlier committee set up to investigate acts of treason and to act as a political police back in 1789. It was renamed in October 1792 with a membership of 30, later reduced to 12 deputies at the beginning of 1793. Its tasks were:

- surveillance over state security
- prosecution of foreign agents and counterfeiters
- regular reporting to the National Convention.

Representatives on mission

Outbreaks of counter-revolutionary violence throughout France prompted the National Convention on 9 March 1793 to send out 82 of its deputies to deal with these problems, a pair to each of the 41 pairs of departments. This was not a new strategy, having similarities to the *intendants* of the Ancien Régime but these representatives on mission had wide ranging powers. Their task in March 1793 was to:

- call local authorities to account for their actions
- restore public order

- arrest suspects (who from 10 March could be sent before the Revolutionary Tribunal)
- check on the functioning of the grain trade
- ensure that the levy for 300,000 men was properly carried out.

On the 9 April representatives on mission were also sent to the armies, three each, to try and make them more effective. These representatives had very wide powers including the power to:

- replace military commanders
- arrest and send individuals to the Revolutionary Tribunal, such as General Houchard who was held responsible for the defeat at Menin and guillotined
- supervise supply and recruitment
- act as a source of propaganda and support the morale of troops
- report daily to the Committee of Public Safety and weekly to the National Convention.

Revolutionary Tribunal

There had been a court specifically to try treasonable offences since 1791 but it was not greatly used. However, the war crisis revived this idea and the threat of violence from the *sans-culottes* made the deputies fearful of a repeat of the September Massacres. On 10 March 1793 the Revolutionary Tribunal was set up to try those accused of counter-revolutionary activities. These included any attempts to re-establish the monarchy, attacks on the principles of the Revolution and attacks on the state's internal and external security. As Danton put it, '… let us be terrible, to dispense the people from the need to be terrible themselves'.

There were five judges (three required for a sentence), a public prosecutor with two assistants and a number of jurymen from Paris and the surrounding departments, all of whom were elected by the National Convention. To begin with, indictments were drawn up by six deputies but from the 5 April this became the responsibility of the public prosecutor.

Committee of Public Safety (CPS)

On the face of it a seemingly innocuous government committee, the Committee of Public Safety became the key to the Terror. It had its origins in earlier attempts to co-ordinate the war effort and was created on 6 April 1793, two days after the treason of General Dumouriez. Dumouriez had tried to lead his army to Paris to overthrow the Convention and when his men refused he defected to the Austrians. The nine members of the CPS were to be elected monthly by the National Convention. Its function was to:

- meet in secret
- supervise the activities of all ministers and agents of the government (this included authority over the Committee of General Security)
- pass decrees collectively relating to 'general defence, external and internal'
- report weekly to the National Convention.

Essentially it was a war cabinet and to begin with it was dominated by Danton whilst Robespierre declined to be a member. He thought it had little usefulness.

The Law of 19 March 1793

This law was a direct response to the widespread revolt in the Vendée region (see page 96). The penalty for any rebel captured carrying arms was death, and with no trial or right of appeal. The majority of executions under the Terror took place under the provision of this law.

Surveillance or Watch committees

Watch committees had their legal origins in August 1792 following the overthrow of the monarchy. The best known were the Watch Committees of the Paris Commune which is often blamed for the September Massacres. On 21 March 1793, in the face of the internal and external threats, a law was passed requiring every commune or town section to set up a watch committee whose members could not be former nobles or churchmen. Their role was to watch foreigners and any involved in riots or conspiracy were to be punished by death. However, the watch committee initially had no powers of arrest. They also issued certificates of *civisme* (civic virtue or support for the Revolution) which all officials had to have.

Stimulus to the Terror – the death of Marat

On the 12 July 1793 Charlotte Corday arrived in Paris from Caen with one purpose in mind: to kill Jean-Paul Marat, the radical journalist and revolutionary firebrand. Marat's journal *L'Ami du peuple* which continually called for violence and his alleged involvement in the September Massacres meant that he was hated by the Girondins. Next morning, a Saturday, she bought a long, black-handled kitchen knife and unsuccessfully tried to see Marat. She left a letter and returned that evening with a second letter asking for his help. This time she promised Marat a list of traitors in the Caen area. This gained her admittance.

Marat suffered from the chronic skin condition psoriasis and spent much of his last three years sitting in his bath, with a vinegar-soaked bandage wrapped around his head and a dressing gown over his shoulders. This gave him relief from the pain and discomfort. This was where Corday found him. As soon as they were alone together she stabbed him, cutting his carotid artery, and he quickly bled to death.

Corday was arrested at the scene and imprisoned. She was tried, convicted and executed on 17 July. She was guillotined in a red dress symbolising patricide. She had killed the 'Father of the People'. During her trial she explained: 'I have killed one man to save one hundred thousand.' She mistakenly believed that Marat's death would end the violence of the Revolution. Instead, Corday's action had the opposite effect. Marat became a revolutionary cult hero and his murder added to the already considerable fear of conspiracy and counter-revolution amongst the leaders of the Revolution. This fear was a major reason why state violence increased rapidly in the period known as the Terror in 1793–94.

Corday herself is omitted from the picture as are the crossed pistols, map of France and painted slogan DEATH with which Marat had decorated his wall to symbolise his desire to kill all enemies of the Revolution.

The tearing gash inflicted by Corday is changed to a delicate incision like those found in paintings of Christ.

David's painting *Marat breathing his last*

Meanwhile Jacques-Louis David had taken on the task of painting Marat. He said, 'Citizens, the people … yearn to see once more the features of their faithful friend. David, they cry, seize your brushes, avenge our friend. Avenge Marat … I heard the voice of the people. I obeyed.' David was well placed. He was a friend of Marat, had visited him the day before his assassination and had access to Marat's corpse. Working quickly he finished the painting in three months. It was exhibited in the courtyard of the Louvre from 14 October and presented to the National Convention in November 1793. Arrangements were made for 1000 printed reproductions to be distributed across France but once again (as they had done when he was painting the *Tennis Court Oath*) events overtook David and the painting was concealed from 1795 until after his death; and it then stayed in Brussels where it remains to this day.

The question for historians of the Revolution is 'what can I learn from this iconic painting?' Simon Schama, historian and art historian, described it as 'airbrushing the revolution'. In contrast, Edgar Wind, an art historian, described it as, 'perhaps the boldest attempt ever made to combine the grandeur of tragedy with the intimacy of portraiture and fuse both in a striking piece of reportage.' If you study the painting for yourself, think about what David included, changed, and omitted. This will enable you to decide which historian's assessment you agree with ('airbrushing' or 'reportage') and whether it is useful evidence for the historian of the Revolution.

In Marat's left hand is Corday's second letter which reads, 'It is enough that I should be quite wretched for me to have a right to your benevolence'. David actually changed her last word which was 'protection' to 'benevolence', thus emphasising Marat's generosity and her treachery. David also has Corday using 'votre' rather than the 'ta' that a citizen would use to link

her with the Ancien Régime even though she too was a revolutionary. Similarly her letter is dated using the Gregorian calendar whilst on the packing case David uses the revolutionary calendar Year Two. This calendar was adopted just days before the painting's completion. In the bottom corners the figures 17 and 93 were painted over.

David portrays Marat with marble-like skin that contrasts starkly with the bloody bath water, not the red flaking skin of psoriasis. His nakedness symbolises his transparency or openness.

For composition purposes David has replaced Marat's shoe shaped bath with a rectangular one. The patched sheet over it is designed to show Marat's self denial.

The packing case desk makes the same point. On it David has placed a note written by Marat. It reads 'you will give this *assignat* to this mother of five children and whose husband died defending his country'.

8 Why did violence increase to become the Terror, 1793–94?

▷ *Camille Desmoulins, his wife Lucile and their baby son Horace, c. 1792, painting, oil on canvas, by Jacques-Louis David.*

Here is a very happy family, Camille Desmoulins, his wife and their baby. Camille was one of the early heroes of the Revolution. A well-known radical journalist, his oratory on that table at the Café Foy is credited by some as triggering the storming of the Bastille in 1789 (see page 45). Yet, less than five brief years later, on 5 April 1794, Camille was guillotined. One week later so was Lucile. His crime was being an 'Indulgent' (see page 61); hers was trying to start a riot at the prison where Camille was held. Both were arrested, tried and executed with the approval of the man who was Camille's old school friend, a guest and witness at their wedding, and godfather to their son Horace, Maximilien Robespierre. It was said that in pleading for Camille's life his mother-in-law asked Robespierre to remember the joy he had felt holding his godson Horace on his knee. But Robespierre was not moved. They both died and little Horace was to grow up an orphan.

Camille and Lucile died during the Terror, the period of little more than a year from spring/summer 1793 through to the coup of Thermidor on 27/28 July 1794. During the Terror many thousands of Frenchmen and women lost their lives, not just in Paris under the guillotine but throughout France in risings against the revolutionary government. This chapter explores the reasons for this rapid escalation of violence, including the role of the man some historians hold responsible – little Horace's godfather, Maximilien Robespierre.

Twelve who ruled – the Committee of Public Safety

During the Terror, France was dominated by the Committee of Public Safety (CPS), set up by the deputies in the National Convention on 6 April 1793. At first it was led by **Danton** but he was replaced after the failure to negotiate an end to the Revolutionary War. By September 1793 the Committee of twelve men who formed what some historians call the 'Great CPS' was in place. It remained in power until the Coup of Thermidor on July 1794.

Its best known and most influential member was **Robespierre**. He provided the main policy link with the National Convention, the Jacobin Club and the Paris Commune and was responsible for policy on religion and with Couthon and Saint-Just major policy strategy and the political police.

Its other members, described by the historian Thomas Carlyle in 1837 as a 'Stranger set of Cloud-Compellers the Earth never saw', and their responsibilities are shown in the table below.

The changes in size (to twelve) and personnel were accompanied by an increase in power. Its roles were to:

- supervise the activities of ministers and agents of the government (including authority over the Committee of General Security)
- pass decrees relating to 'general defence, external and internal' and conduct foreign policy
- report weekly to the National Convention
- issue arrest warrants for suspects
- nominate the membership of the Committee of General Security
- exercise authority over all ministers, generals and representatives on mission and could replace officials with its own nominees.

The Committee met in a room at the Tuileries, once Louis XVI's private office. It had 50 million livres for secret expenses but historians are unsure exactly how it operated. The position is best outlined by Roy Palmer, author of *Twelve Who Ruled: The Year of the Terror in the French Revolution* (1941).

> Make sure you have read pages 76–77 on **Danton** and **Robespierre** before reading further.

	Responsible for:
Saint-Just	war organisation and, with Robespierre, major policy strategy and political police
Couthon	with Robespierre major policy strategy and political police
Barère	liaison with the National Convention, education, diplomacy
Billaud-Varenne	correspondence with representatives on mission
Collot-d'Herbois	correspondence with representatives on mission
Lindet	food supply
Carnot	war strategy and personnel
Prieur de la Côte-d'Or	war industries
Saint André	navy
Prieur de la Marne	usually on mission
Hérault de Séchelles	diplomacy

The Committee transacted its affairs at all hours, but its real sessions took place secretly, behind closed doors, at night. No one knows exactly what happened at such conclaves. Anyone interested today can read, in large clear print, thousands of documents emanating from the Committee, ordinances, proclamations, letters of command, advice and instruction. No one can say what passed over the green table before the decisions were reached. No evidence for these matters exists except a few contemporary innuendos made for political purposes, a few indiscretions, a great many rumours, and a few recollections written down years later by two or three of the survivors. But the debates were undoubtedly lively, and the Twelve had many secrets. They fought and disputed with each other, sometimes differing widely in policy, their nerves on edge from sheer fatigue, their minds inflamed by revolutionary passions.

How many people died in the Terror?

The timeline with bar graph summarises the Terror and places it in the context of the civil and Revolutionary Wars. Arriving at a precise figure for the total number of deaths in this period is difficult. Those tried by the Revolutionary Tribunal and other courts can be accurately counted because trials and executions were properly recorded. The figures in each bar give a total of 16,770 people sentenced to death by the various courts. It's more difficult to know numbers for those who died awaiting trial or release. Estimates suggest up to 12,000 out of roughly half a million people who were at some point held in prison accused of revolutionary offences died.

In addition between 10,000 and 12,000 people were executed without a trial during the civil wars under the Law of 19 March 1793. There were also those killed in the rising in the Vendée, the atrocities committed there by both sides and the resulting hunger and epidemic disease. Francois Lebrun (1986) places this death toll at between 150,000 and 200,000 people.

Finally there were the soldiers who were killed in battle, died from wounds or were killed by epidemic diseases. On the timeline, just the reported casualties in the major battles are shown. From the statistics below it is clear that just the major battles in the war against the First Coalition (see page 98) were responsible for the deaths of more than 30,000 Frenchmen. The historian Colin Jones actually gives a figure of 203,000 for the years 1792–94.

▽ French deaths during the Revolution. (All figures on pp.96–97 from *The Longman Companion to the French Revolution* by Colin Jones, Pearson Education Limited © Longman Group UK Limited 1988.)

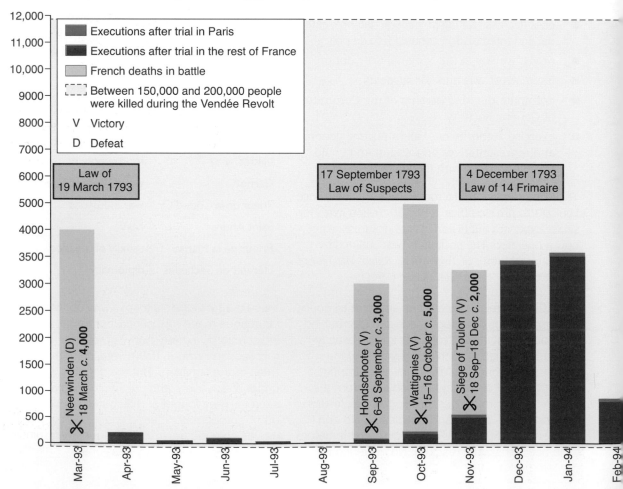

One of the stereotypes surrounding the French Revolution is that it was mostly the aristocrats who 'Kissed Madam Guillotine', but as the pie charts on the right show this was definitely not the case. The graphs are based upon the figures of Donald Greer (1935) for the provinces and of J L Godfrey (1951) for Paris. Qualifying the implications of the figures on which these charts are based, the historian Louis Henry (1964) pointed out that the aristocracy represented less than one per cent of the French population whilst the peasantry represented more than 70 per cent. Nevertheless this does not nullify Greer's conclusion from the figures that the Terror cannot be interpreted in class terms.

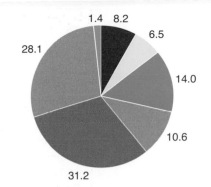

△ Pie chart 1 showing the social class of the victims for France as a whole. This in part helps to explain the large percentage of peasants executed.

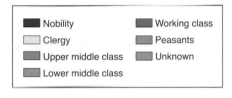

Legend:
- Nobility
- Clergy
- Upper middle class
- Lower middle class
- Working class
- Peasants
- Unknown

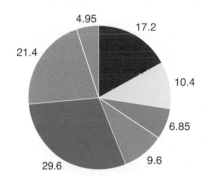

△ Pie chart 2 showing the social class of the 1314 female victims of the Terror for France as a whole. This suggests that whilst aristocratic women suffered commensurately more than their menfolk in other social classes the same was not the case.

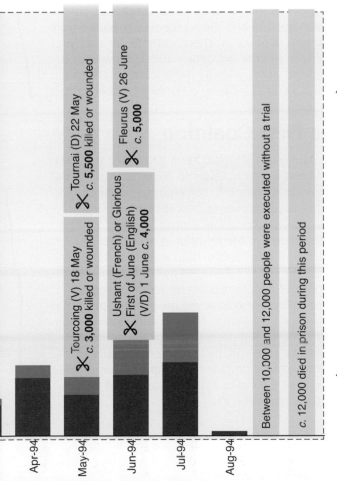

Apr-94

Tourcoing (V) 18 May ✗ c. 3,000 killed or wounded

Tournai (D) 22 May ✗ c. 5,500 killed or wounded

May-94

Ushant (French) or Glorious First of June (English) (V/D) 1 June c. 4,000 ✗

Fleurus (V) 26 June ✗ c. 5,000

Jun-94

Jul-94

Aug-94

Between 10,000 and 12,000 people were executed without a trial

c. 12,000 died in prison during this period

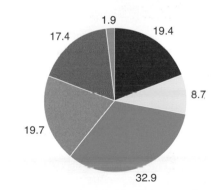

△ Pie chart 3 showing the social class of the victims of the Paris Revolutionary Tribunal. The greater percentage of aristocrats executed in Paris may suggest one possible reason for the development of the stereotype detailed above.

The situation in 1793

The **First Coalition** was prompted by the execution of Louis XVI and was heavily influenced by British diplomacy and subsidies. Austria, Britain, Portugal, Holland, Prussia, Russia, Sardinia and Spain made up the First Coalition.

The problems facing the Committee of Public Safety in 1793 which will be examined in this chapter were immense. On its borders France's armies faced the Austrian, British, Dutch, Portuguese, Prussian, Sardinian and Spanish armies of the **First Coalition**. The war effort required to meet this threat was huge plus there were food shortages and inflation. There were also internal revolts and rebellions to deal with. Moreover the revolutionaries themselves in the CPS and the National Convention were not all in agreement about how to proceed. There were the idealists and the pragmatists, the moderates and the extremists and all knew that if they and the Revolution failed then they would die as criminals, murderers of their king. And they lived in fear of plots by *émigrés* and other political factions and in fear of personal attack.

War against the First Coalition

At the end of 1792 the Revolutionary War had been going well for France. The Prussian advance had been halted at Valmy in September 1792 and the Prussians then withdrew from France. In November, French armies defeated the Austrians at Jemappes. However, success ended in early 1793 as the First Coalition came into existence. Once again war had a major impact upon France and the course of the Revolution. By February 1793 France was under attack from all sides (as the map shows) and the reputation of the pro war Girondins was damaged by the war going badly and by the negative economic effects, which in turn led to increased militancy amongst the *sans-culottes* who attacked the printing presses of Girondin newspapers in Paris on 9/10 March. Soon British, Austrian and Spanish troops were on French soil and there were real fears that the Austrians would march on Paris. However, by September the tide of the war had turned, partly because the countries of the First Coalition did not act together but instead pursued their own individual aims and partly because of the actions of the Committee itself.

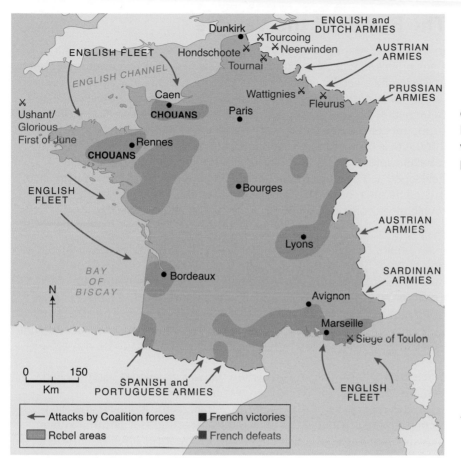

ENGLISH and
DUTCH ARMIES
Dunkirk
✕Tourcoing
ENGLISH FLEET   Hondschoote   ✕Neerwinden
AUSTRIAN
ARMIES
Tournai
ENGLISH CHANNEL
Wattignies✕   PRUSSIAN
Caen   Fleurus   ✕ARMIES
Ushant/   CHOUANS   Paris
Glorious
First of June   ●Rennes
CHOUANS
ENGLISH
FLEET
●Bourges
AUSTRIAN
ARMIES
●Lyons
SARDINIAN
ARMIES
BAY
OF   ●Bordeaux
N   BISCAY
Avignon
Marseille
✕ Siege of Toulon
0   150
Km
SPANISH and
PORTUGUESE ARMIES   ENGLISH
FLEET

← Attacks by Coalition forces   ■ French victories
▨ Rebel areas   ■ French defeats

Chouans
Royalist insurgents who
were mainly peasants (see
page 120)

◁ **The threats to France
from external attacks
and internal revolts.**

Carnot was responsible for the decree of 23 August 1793 that ordered the
levée en masse. All unmarried men between the ages of 18 and 25 were
called for military service. This produced an army of almost 800,000 by
early 1794. The rest of the population was also affected with men drawn
into a massively expanded munitions industry, food production and
transport for the war effort. Women were expected to staff hospitals and
make clothes. The Committee also dispatched representatives on mission
to the armies, notably Carnot and Saint-Just to improve army morale and
effectiveness. They were also sent to supervise the generals as the
defections of Dumouriez and Lafayette meant that the other Generals were
not entirely trusted. Later in 1793 Generals Custine and Houchard were
recalled and guillotined.

In October 1793 the army drove the Austrians out of France. In
December Toulon was recaptured and the British fleet driven out, thanks
to the actions of the young commander of artillery, Napoleon Bonaparte
and the now strong French armies won a decisive victory at Fleurus in the
Netherlands on 26 June 1794. From then on the French remained on the
offensive until all their opponents had been knocked out of the war.

■ **Think about**
Which aspects of
war may have
prompted opposition
to the Revolution
amongst some
French people?

99

The Revolt of the Vendée

In the early days of March 1793 the revolutionary government's call to arms provoked violence in the Vendée. The first riots occurred on 4 March at Cholet, followed by attacks on supporters and officials of the Revolution and seizures of their weapons. On 11 March the towns of Machecoul and Bourgneuf were over-run by armed rebels and between 300 and 500 supporters of the Revolution were massacred. The next day more than 2000 rebels captured St Florent and other towns were attacked. As the rebellion spread, more towns were captured as larger rebel groups developed, led by ex-professional soldiers. A number of nobles were also invited by the rebels to become leaders. By the 19 March worried local revolutionary officials sent their report to the Minister of War.

> Our affairs on the left bank of the Loire are in much worse shape. The districts of St Florent, Choloe and Vihiers pillaged, ravaged and burned, more than five hundred patriots slaughtered in these different cities. Two formidable columns of rebels led by experienced men are marching en masse on Saumur and Angers. The little army we put into the field tried in vain to battle that enormous mass. It was forced to retreat rapidly to Ponts-de-Ce in order not to be cut off.

The arrival of this news in Paris when the war was going badly fuelled deputies' fears that the Revolution was in great danger.

In this first phase of the revolt the Vendeans mostly used guerrilla tactics but the combined Catholic and Royal army, as it became known, did win battles against revolutionary troops by sheer force of numbers. At Pont-Charrault on 19 March 2000 revolutionary troops were routed and on 22 March near Chalonnes 300 revolutionary troops fled from an estimated 20,000 Vendean rebels. Between April and June rebels took control of the Vendée and fought a largely defensive campaign. They did capture and sack the cities of Saumur and Angers, and also Thouars and Fontenay though without attempting to permanently occupy them.

The debate over why the revolt broke out illustrates how historians can differ and what can happen when a **sociologist**, in this case Charles Tilly, gets involved. The traditional view was that the revolt was simply one of peasants opposed to the Revolution and motivated by royalism (they were oppressed by the Revolution and shocked by the execution of the King), resistance to conscription, religion (they were loyal to the Catholic Church or to their parish priest or curé), the self interest of their leaders and their uncritical loyalty.

In his book *The Vendée* (1964) Tilly argued that such sweeping statements about the motives of peasants were inadequate. What was needed was to explore in depth the people involved on both sides in order to explain why this revolt occurred in some places but not others. He took a sociologist's approach to the question and after many years of archival research in the Mauges area reached a number of conclusions. First, that it was a struggle between the counter-revolutionary countryside and the revolutionary towns. Second, that the lines of division were not horizontal but vertical and that peasants, bourgeois and aristocrats could be found on

sociology
This is the study of the development, structure and functioning of human society

both sides. Third, that a sociological perspective can help to refine historical questions, something that many social historians would agree with. And for his last conclusion I'll let Tilly's words speak for him.

Finally, 'What turned the people of the Mauges against the Revolution?' still seems worth asking, but with very important provisos that no single factor, policy, motive, or group can be the answer; that one must ask which people turned, how much, and how; that firm answers can only come from systematic tests of proposed explanations in areas which did not turn against the Revolution.

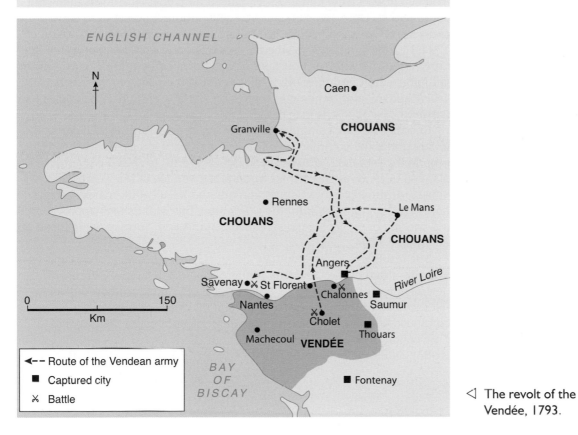

◁ The revolt of the Vendée, 1793.

The Committee saw defeat of the rebels as crucial to the survival of the Revolution. In a speech to the National Convention Barère said: 'Destroy the Vendée and Valenciennes will no longer be in Austrian hands. Destroy the Vendée and the Prussians will no longer hold the Rhine. Destroy the Vendée and the English will no longer occupy Dunkirk.' Therefore additional resources were allocated to the campaign and these bore fruit in October when the rebels were defeated at Cholet. Roughly 60,000 rebels, men, women and children escaped and headed for the port of Granville where they hoped to rendezvous with a British fleet carrying reinforcements and supplies. They failed to capture the port and the British fleet did not materialise so the rebels retreated back south. Weakened by hunger and disease they failed to capture Angers, were defeated at Le Mans in December and the survivors wiped out at Savenay.

■ **Think about**
- What measures were taken to put down the revolt?
- Which factors explain the severity of punishments?

In the aftermath, thousands of rebels were imprisoned and tried by military commissions. Under the Law of 19 March armed rebels could be executed within 24 hours of capture. Military commissions sat in judgement, simply verifying a person's identity and then passing sentence of death. Over 8700 people were executed, the greatest numbers in Nantes. Most were shot by firing squads in quarries outside the town.

The representative on mission in the area was Jean-Baptiste Carrier. He became notorious for the brutality of his treatment of rebels. The *noyades* were deliberate drownings of people in the River Loire. They were done in secrecy, at night, with no records being kept. They began on 16 November when 90 priests were tied together, placed on a boat which was taken out onto the river Loire and sunk. At least seven more *noyades* were carried out and several thousand people died before they were stopped in January 1794. Historians differ as to whether this was done with the approval of the Committee and whether Robespierre was horrified by these events. Carrier did inform the Committee what he was doing but used phrases such as 'civic baptism' and 'sending to Nantes by water'. Certainly Robespierre had Carrier recalled to Paris in February 1794 to answer for his actions.

Guerrilla fighting continued after the Vendean armies were destroyed. In December the commander of the revolutionary forces, General Turreau, proposed a scorched earth policy to the CPS to try to stop the guerrillas. He planned to send his two armies through the Vendée to burn crops and houses, destroy livestock and equipment and kill all adult males. Despite not receiving any reply from the Committee but with its tacit approval and the backing of the local representatives on mission, Turreau went ahead on 20 January 1794.

The result was a humanitarian disaster. The troops were undisciplined and also afraid of the Vendeans so there was murder, rape, looting and destruction on a vast scale. As a result local resistance increased. People felt they had nothing to lose. A campaign that was planned to last a week continued with great ferocity until the end of April when the National Convention ordered it stopped. Thousands died. As you saw earlier, Lebrun (1986) places the final death toll at between 150,000 and 200,000.

▷ *Noyades dans la Loire par ordre du péroce Carrier*, an engraving by Pierre Berthault. This was one of 123 plates in his pro revolutionary publication, 'Tableaux Historiques de la Révolution Française'.

The purge of the Girondins/*Journée* of 2 June 1793

◁ *Arrestation des deputés Girondins – les Tuileries encerclées par la Garde Nationale, 2 Juin 1793*, an engraving by Pierre Berthault. Although the National Guard point their cannons at the National Convention this *journée* was in fact non violent.

The war against the First Coalition and the civil war in the Vendée were not the only wars fought in 1793. There was a third war, a political war between the Girondins and the Montagnards and if the fighting was carried out with words rather than swords then the consequences of defeat were just as deadly. The two sides had disagreed over the fate of Louis and each saw the other as conspiring against the Revolution.

The Girondins were hampered because they had promoted the war and were blamed for its failures and its negative economic impacts, most importantly a fall in the value of *assignat* which made food more expensive. The loss of colonial markets through the English naval blockade and rising unemployment in luxury trades contributed to *sans-culotte* dissatisfaction. The Paris sections called for price controls on basic commodities, a demand which the National Convention refused. Then there were disturbances in Paris in February over bread and soap prices which the National Guard brought under control. The Girondins had support in the provinces where the policies of leading Montagnards like Robespierre and Marat were viewed as too extreme but the Montagnards had support from the *sans-culottes* in Paris who saw them as realists who were willing to take the harsh measures required to protect the Revolution. The Girondins on the other hand attacked the *sans-culottes* as *buveurs de sang* (drinkers of blood).

In April the Girondins went on the offensive against the Montagnards. They blamed the February disturbances on Marat and on 12 April called for him to be impeached (charged with crimes against the state). They were successful in getting him taken before the Revolutionary Tribunal but Marat was acquitted and carried back in triumph to the National Convention by thousands of his *sans-culotte* supporters. One major consequence of the impeachment was that 8000 demonstrators surrounded the National Convention on 3 May demanding price controls on bread. Significantly the Montagnards had moved from opposing to supporting price controls. The next day a law setting a maximum price for grain and bread was passed.

> **Think about**
> - What determined each side's support?
> - Why were these events likely to lead to political violence?

The struggle for control within the National Convention continued. Messages of support for the Girondins came from the provinces but plans for a purge of Girondin deputies by the *sans-culottes* were developing. At the Jacobin Club on 26 May Robespierre called for an insurrection against the 'corrupt deputies' of the National Convention. The Montagnards had allied themselves with the *sans-culottes*.

On 31 May the first insurrection failed but two days later the National Convention was surrounded by 100,000 National Guards demanding the arrest of 29 Girondins deputies. When the National Convention deputies tried to leave they were all physically stopped so, in order to avoid its armed overthrow, they put the matter to a vote. Although many deputies abstained, enough, including the Montagnards, voted to have the Girondins arrested (see page 106 on their trial and execution). The result was that the National Convention continued to rule, with power in the hands of the Montagnards. The price they paid was that they were dependent on the *sans-culottes* and had had to accept the use of armed force against an elected assembly.

Federalist revolts

On 29 May 1793 Lyons overthrew its Jacobin rulers and in reaction to the purge of the Girondins on 2 June other cities, notably Avignon, Bordeaux, Caen, Marseilles and Toulon revolted too. Their motives were a mixture of resentment of the influence of the Paris Commune on the course of the Revolution and support for the Girondins. In time the character of these revolts changed from **federalism** to counter-revolution in Lyons and Toulon.

Although these revolts posed a potentially significant threat to the Revolution, the cities were never able to work together. They had few troops, which reflected a lack of popular support, and they were unwilling to advance far from their homes. This enabled the French army to defeat each revolt separately. Between July and October each city was taken, culminating in the capture of Lyons after a two-month siege.

federalism

In this context, federalism meant local areas/ departments having an influence on the course of the Revolution and having some independence in running their own affairs

In the aftermath representatives on mission were responsible for administering revolutionary justice. Robespierre noted that what was needed was, 'making a terrible example of all the criminals who have outraged liberty and spilt the blood of patriots'. An example was made of Lyons, where leading Jacobins had been guillotined by the rebels. Many of the houses of the richer rebels were destroyed and the representative on mission, Couthon, set up a popular justice court, executing 113 rebels in six weeks but that was not considered to be enough by his colleagues in the Committee. He was replaced in November by Collot d'Herbois and Joseph Fouché. They set up a revolutionary commission which sentenced 1673 people to death, and the departmental criminal court sentenced a further 213 to death.

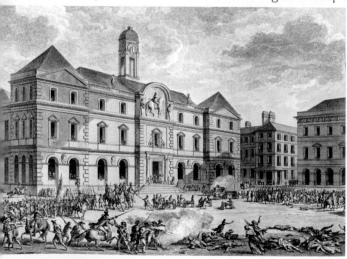

△ *Mitraillades de Lyons, Commandées par Collot d'Herbois*, an engraving by Pierre Berthault.

To speed up the process and to shock the local population, on 4 and 5 December, in the **mitraillades** prisoners were lined up in front of cannons and mown down by grape shot (hundreds of small iron balls). Many were wounded and had to be finished off by hand. The soldiers were not happy doing this and thereafter executions were carried out by guillotine or firing squads.

mitraillades
Mass execution by cannon fire

Pressure for more terror

The Committee also faced political and economic demands from the *sans-culottes* who had put them in power. One consequence of the war was inflation and the falling value of the *assignat* hit the poorer sections of society hardest. The *sans-culottes* wanted action on food supplies and for prices to be set that could be afforded by ordinary people. The Committee did not want to do this. They believed in a free market economy but did accept that in wartime special measures were necessary. In May 1793 they imposed price controls on grain but this backfired as farmers sold their grain on the black market so that supplies of grain to Paris fell and bread prices rose. The *sans-culottes* then called for terror to be used against farmers and grain merchants. The Committee responded with a law making hoarding grain a capital offence and by setting up public granaries to manage the supply. Neither worked.

By August the *assignat* was worth less than a third of its face value and drought had further reduced grain supplies to Paris. It was then that extremists, the *Enragés* (angry men) emerged. Men such as Jacques Roux called for higher taxes on the rich, death for hoarders and the arrest of political suspects, in short more terror. The journalist Hébert demanded similar measures in his newspaper *Père Duchesne*. Both were critical of the government and very influential with the *sans-culottes*. The pressure built up until on 5 September thousands of *sans-culottes* surrounded the National Convention. They demanded the formation of a *sans-culotte* revolutionary army to track down hoarders and arrest political suspects. The deputies agreed and the *sans-culottes* dispersed. With the *sans-culottes* placated, the CPS could move against Roux – he was arrested and later committed suicide. However, the Paris revolutionary army, over 7000 strong, was set up and given the task of patrolling the departments around Paris. Other revolutionary armies sprang up in the provinces. Moreover, on 29 September a '**general maximum**' was passed to enforce wage and price controls throughout France.

These concessions ensured that, despite the power of the *sans-culottes*, the National Convention and the Committee stayed in control. However, the deputies now accepted that more extreme measures were needed to preserve the Revolution. Terror was the 'order of the day'.

Added to this hardening of attitudes was the revolutionaries' very real fear of personal attack. In January 1793 the Jacobin Lepeletier had been assassinated and in July, so was Marat (see page 92). One Jacobin claimed Paris was full of assassins, 'monsters foaming with rage, who are only waiting for the favourable moment to fall on patriots and cut their throats'. As men of the people they could not surround themselves with bodyguards like Kings so they felt vulnerable.

Think about
Which factors contributed to the severity of the punishments of Federalist rebels?

general maximum
Maximum was a set of price fixing regulations, passed first in May 1793 to fix the highest permitted price of grain and then in the 'general maximum' this was applied to all items that were essentials of life

The Political Terror

In response to *sans-culotte* pressure the National Convention passed another measure on 17 September 1793, the Law of Suspects. This widened the definition of who was 'against the Revolution' to include royalists and federalists, relations of *émigrés*, anyone without a certificate of *civisme* from their local watch committee or without a visible source of income and anyone dismissed from government office. The watch committees were to arrest all these suspects and send details of charges to the Committee of General Security. The numbers in prison rose dramatically so the Paris Revolutionary Tribunal was expanded into four sections, two sitting at any one time.

The pace of convictions and executions accelerated but in roughly half of the Revolutionary Tribunal's cases the accused were acquitted. Between March and September 70 people in total had been guillotined in Paris. During October, November and December the pace increased and a total of 178 were guillotined (see pages 96–97). After the first of a series of show trials Marie Antoinette went to the guillotine on the 16 October but the key event was the trial of twenty-one Girondins, including Brissot, which began on 24 October. The Girondins still enjoyed some support and as their trial carried on for five days an acquittal began to look increasingly likely. So Robespierre intervened in the National Convention to propose that if after three days a jury were convinced that the accused were guilty then they could return a guilty verdict straight away. The deputies of the National Convention voted in favour of this speeding up of trials. The Girondins were convicted and went, singing *La Marseillaise*, to the guillotine on 31 October. In a classical reference to the Roman God Saturn eating his own children one Girondin, Pierre Vergniaud, commented 'the Revolution, like Saturn, devours its children'.

A number of other prominent revolutionaries went to the guillotine in the following months. Amongst them were Philippe Égalité (arrested after his son defected to the Austrians along with General Dumouriez), Madam Roland, Bailly, the ex-mayor of Paris held responsible for the Champ de Mars massacre, General Houchard, Barnave the early hero of the Tennis Court Oath and a prominent Feuillant and finally Madam du Barry, once mistress of Louis XV.

'Religious terror'

Another aspect of the Revolution was de-Christianisation, the 'religious terror' which was driven by the *sans-culottes*, the revolutionary armies and some representatives on mission such as Fouché rather than the National Convention. Hatred of the Catholic Church led to the closure of churches, the removal of church bells and the destruction of roadside shrines. Some priests (estimates vary from 6000 to 20,000) were forced to give-up their priesthood. This religious terror spread throughout France by early 1794.

The Dictatorship of the Committee of Public Safety

By the end of 1793 it was clear that the policies of the Jacobin government were successful. Revolts had been defeated and foreign troops driven from France. It was then possible for the CPS to assert control over the *sans-culottes*,

△ *Marie Antoinette Led to her Execution*. After making this pen and ink sketch, 15x10 cm, Jacques-Louis David went on to the official unveiling of his *Marat breathing his last* (see page 93).

■ Think about

Why did each of the following increase demands for terror?

- Economic factors
- Personal fears
- The power of the *sans-culottes*

a process begun back in September when the National Convention had decreed that the sections of the Paris Commune should only meet twice a week. This limited the ability of *sans-culottes* to organise and influence events. Then, in October the National Convention passed a decree that suspended the Constitution with its one man one vote.

Finally the Law of Frimaire on 4 December 1793 established Revolutionary Government. This confirmed that between them the CGS and the CPS had full executive powers including control of representatives on mission and crucially of local government. This enabled the CPS to break the power of the *sans-culottes* in the Paris Commune. This law also disbanded all revolutionary armies except the one in Paris. It went back on all the earlier revolutionary ideals of decentralisation of government, the separation of the legislative and the executive and the provision of impartial justice. The Jacobin government was now a dictatorship. Robespierre justified this saying, 'We must organise the despotism of liberty to crush the despotism of kings'.

As 1793 drew to an end the Committee of Public Safety found itself challenged by two factions. Moderates, the Indulgents, led by Danton wanted an end to the Terror but the radicals led by Hébert were calling for an escalation of the Terror with more executions of hoarders and the redistribution of property. Hébert was also an enthusiastic supporter of de-Christianisation. This was something which Robespierre opposed and he persuaded the National Convention to confirm the principle of religious freedom.

The destruction of the Hébertists and the Indulgents

In December 1793 Camille Desmoulins returned to political prominence, publishing a newspaper, the *Vieux Cordelier*, to campaign for the end of the Terror. In the first two editions (which were approved by Robespierre) Desmoulins attacked political extremists, namely Hébert and his supporters. Briefly it seemed that moderation would triumph over extremism, especially when the National Convention ordered the arrest of two Hébertist extremists. Robespierre also talked of setting up a clemency committee to consider the cases against all political prisoners. But at this point Collot d'Herbois (back in Paris to answer criticism of his harsh repression in Lyons) argued that terror was needed and condemned the arrest of the Hébertists. When Billaud-Varenne also challenged the idea of a clemency committee Robespierre immediately withdrew his support for the Indulgents' campaign for moderation. He then made a speech to the National Convention condemning both moderates and extremists. Next day the clemency committee was disbanded.

The Indulgents' campaign was also hit by suspicions of corruption surrounding some of them, including Danton, and suggestions that they wanted to end the Terror to protect themselves. By now, Robespierre and the CPS saw signs of conspiracy everywhere. He viewed both factions as threats to the Jacobin government and to the survival of the Revolution. In a speech to the National Convention on 5 February 1794 he justified the Terror like this:

> If the mainspring of popular government in peacetime is virtue, the mainspring of popular government in revolution is virtue and terror both: virtue, without which terror is disastrous; terror, without which virtue is powerless. Terror is nothing but prompt, severe, inflexible justice; it is therefore an emanation of virtue; it is not so much a specific principle as a consequence of the general principle of democracy applied to the homeland's most pressing needs.

Meanwhile the search for evidence against both factions went on. In February the Hébertists were released and, determined on revenge, they accused both the Indulgents and the CPS of betraying the Revolution and called for a popular uprising but failed to mobilise *sans-culotte* support. However, with unrest among *sans-culottes* increasing due to food shortages, the CPS knew it had to act swiftly. On 13 March, Saint-Just accused the Hébertists of being part of a foreign plot against the Revolution. Next day the leading Hébertists were arrested and taken before the Revolutionary Tribunal, accused of plotting to starve Paris, planning a military dictatorship and of handing over France to its enemies. Though these charges were not true they were found guilty and guillotined. Despite their popularity there was little public protest and the CPS took the opportunity to disband the Paris revolutionary army and close the clubs and societies in which the *sans-culottes* met. The job was finished with the replacement of Hébert's supporters on the Paris Commune by Robespierre's.

That left the Indulgents and their call for an end to the Terror. They were far more of a threat because Danton had so much support in the National Convention. As Marc-Antoine Vadier, a member of the Committee of General Security warned: 'If we do not guillotine them they will guillotine us'. Most members of the CPS wanted to move against Danton and the Indulgents but Robespierre did not. Historians believe that the two men met on 22 March. Here is how historian Ruth Scurr describes the climactic moment.

> He [Robespierre] went to a dinner at which Danton was also a guest. Robespierre seemed silent and agitated. Bold as ever, Danton asked him directly why there were still so many victims of the Terror: 'Royalists and conspirators I can understand, but what about those who are innocent?' 'And who says anyone innocent has perished?' Robespierre retorted coldly.

Whatever else was said the two men failed to reach an agreement and that night Robespierre signed the arrest warrant for Danton, Desmoulins and the other leading Indulgents. Their trial began on 2 April. They were accused of conspiring to overthrow the Committee of Public Safety and the Committee of General Security. Danton, one of the great heroes of the Revolution, was so successful in defending himself that, fearing an acquittal, the CPS rushed through a new decree that anyone who insulted the justice system could be removed from court. Danton and his co-defendants were then removed before they could finish their defence. They were found guilty, sentenced to death and went to the guillotine next day, 5 April 1794. With them went a moderate member of the CPS, Hérault de Séchelles, also convicted of conspiracy. Now no one could feel safe. The revolutionaries saw conspiracy everywhere. It was no coincidence that in the Jacobin Club that night Robespierre insisted that they discuss conspiracy.

Think about

What evidence is there on pages 106–108 of the CPS acting to protect the Revolution?

The Great Terror

The period that followed in Paris is known as the Great Terror. Ironically, just as Charlotte Corday's effort to stop the Terror by killing Marat had the opposite effect so too did the Indulgents' attempt. Following the fall of

Danton no one dared challenge the CPS. Its eleven surviving members pushed ahead with centralising control and repression. They brought in a number of significant pieces of legislation.

The law of 27 Germinal Year II (16 April 1794) **Law on General Police** banned former nobles and foreigners from living in ports and frontier towns. It allowed the CPS to set up a police bureau to root out counter-revolutionaries in the administration, soon broadened out to recruit agents to identify suspects all over France. It was run by Saint-Just and, when he went on mission in May, by Robespierre. It was soon sending suspects, mostly nobles and clergy suspected of counter-revolutionary plotting and ex-Hébertists, to the Revolutionary Tribunal.

The law of 19 Floréal Year II (8 May 1794) gave the **Paris Revolutionary Tribunal** jurisdiction over all counter-revolutionary offences and most other revolutionary courts were shut down.

In May 1794 came two more assassination attempts. In the first a man called 'Admiral' waited in a stairwell to get a shot at Robespierre and then shot at Collot d'Herbois but the only person hurt was a bystander who tried to help. Five days later a young woman, Cécile Renault, called to see Robespierre at his lodging. Seen acting suspiciously, she was found to be carrying a fruit knife. Although it is disputed whether she actually intended to assassinate Robespierre she was guillotined, wearing a red dress like Charlotte Corday.

The **Law of 22 Prairial Year II** (10 June 1794) was drafted by Robespierre and Couthon to expand the definition of political crimes to include 'criticism of patriotism' and 'perverting public opinion'. It made guilty verdicts far more likely as it abolished both defence counsels and public cross-examination of defendants. It decreed that defence witnesses did not have to be heard, that evidence of guilt could be 'moral' as well as material and that the only verdicts the Tribunal could reach were death or acquittal. Under this law the acquittal rate dropped to 20 per cent while the use of batch trials, where groups of defendants were tried together on the same charge, speeded things up. Unsurprisingly the numbers guillotined rose rapidly.

	Number guillotined
April 1794	244
May 1794	339
June 1794	659
July 1794	935
August 1794	6

△ Victims of the Great Terror.

The reasons for the Great Terror

Historians have disagreed about why the Great Terror occurred. Some simply blamed it on Robespierre, pointing to the fact that he drafted The Law of 22 Prairial. Left wing historians who wanted to defend Robespierre saw the roots of the Great Terror in a war against the rich, pointing to earlier legislation which decreed that the property of those convicted should be redistributed amongst the poor. However, there is little evidence that this was happening at the time. Another suggestion is that the Great Terror was a direct response to the assassination attempts on Robespierre and Collot d'Herbois but at the time these were not mentioned.

The historian Hugh Gough (2010) suggests the most convincing explanation is that it was part of the policy of centralisation. In order to avoid local courts being too lenient, suspects were sent to Paris, but then in order to deal with prison overcrowding the trial process needed to be speeded up. As the CPS believed the suspects were guilty anyway there was little purpose to long trials. This argument is the most convincing, if chilling.

> ■ **Think about**
> Which factors help to explain the laws of 1794 and the increase in deaths during the Great Terror?

Robespierre and the Terror – why was he overthrown?

The Terror came to an abrupt end in the chaotic bloodbath of Thermidor in July 1794. On 9 Thermidor Robespierre tried to address the National Convention but was shouted down. He had lost control of the deputies and the National Convention ordered that Robespierre and his close associates on the CPS Couthon and Saint-Just were arrested. His brother Augustin and friend Philippe Lebas insisted on being arrested with him. Finally, the commander of the Paris National Guard, Hanriot, was also arrested. Later that day they all escaped arrest and went to the Paris Commune at the Hotel de Ville. Here they unsuccessfully tried to rally their supporters against those of the National Convention. Their initial National Guard supporters melted away and when the Convention's forces arrived they arrested Robespierre for a second time, as Harriet depicts in the picture below. Now Robespierre and his supporters, including the entire Paris Commune, had become armed rebels and that afternoon, after simply being identified, they went to the guillotine. The whole process had taken less than 24 hours.

△ *The night of the 9/10 Thermidor, Year 2, the Arrest of Robespierre* colour engraving by Jean-Joseph-François Tassaert (1765–c.1835) after a painting by Fulchran-Jean Harriet (1776–1805) a former pupil of Jacques-Louis David. It shows gendarme Charles-André Merda firing the shot which he claimed broke Robespierre's jaw. Other versions of this event say Robespierre fired the shot whilst attempting suicide.

There were a number of reasons for Robespierre's fall. He had been ill, perhaps through overwork or a nervous breakdown and had not been attending meetings of the Committee of Public Safety and the National Convention. He had quarrelled with some of the other CPS members, both moderates and extremists and with the Committee of General Security members who saw his work as head of the police bureau as impinging upon their authority. He also had more long-standing quarrels with the supporters of de-Christianisation and the terrorists amongst the representatives on mission, notably Fouché. Additionally his recent role as high priest of the **Cult of the Supreme Being** had made him a figure of ridicule rather than enhancing his status. However, the main factor in his fall was fear.

The day before his arrest in a long, rambling speech to the National Convention Robespierre had said there was a 'conspiracy against public liberty' that involved deputies, the Committee of General Security and even members of the Committee of Public Safety. Robespierre had promised to name those conspirators. Moderates and **terrorists** alike feared it might be them so they combined against him accusing him of dictatorship. Robespierre found that his *sans-culottes* supporters did nothing to save him. Were the *sans-culottes* now too weak or was it their anger at the new wage maximum scale (see page 105) which threatened to reduce their wages? For the deputies, Baudot commented on their motives, 'Principles had nothing to do with it, it was a matter of killing.' Immediately afterwards the surviving members of the CPS tried to continue the Terror issuing many arrest warrants against Robespierre's supporters; but the deputies of the National Convention reasserted their control and ended the Terror.

Was Robespierre to blame?

Those who overthrew Robespierre were quick to put the blame for everything on him, men like Fouché who had been so ferocious as a representative on mission now reinvented themselves (Fouché went on to become a Duke under Napoleon).

The case against Robespierre is certainly strong. From 1791 he had come to dominate and lead the Jacobin Club; and its influence on the government of revolutionary France was undeniable. He was also the one who saw the need for *sans-culottes* support to overthrow the monarchy. When the Insurrectionary Committee plotted the decisive *journée* of 10 August 1792 he was certainly consulted, and he spoke out in public on 29 July calling for direct action.

Like others his role in the September Massacres was unclear. He was present at a meeting of the Insurrectionary Committee on 2 September when news of the first killings at the Abbaye prison came in. His only interventions, according to Ruth Scurr, were to check on the security of the royal family imprisoned in the Temple and to try and get his political enemies Brissot and Roland arrested. This would almost certainly have resulted in their deaths but was blocked by Danton.

Robespierre's intentions were certainly mistrusted by the Girondin deputies, led by Brissot and Roland, who accused him of dictatorial tendencies in the National Convention in late September 1792. The bitter struggle between them ended in the *journée* of 2 June 1793 when, with *sans-culottes* support, the Girondins were arrested. Their trials and deaths followed.

The **Cult of the Supreme Being** was set up by a decree of the National Convention on 7 May 1794 following a speech on political morality by Robespierre. It recognised the existence of a supreme being and the immortality of the soul. Robespierre was anxious to halt the de-Christianisation campaigns led by the Paris Commune and the Hébertists.

terrorist
This was a term used retrospectively to describe those involved in perpetrating the Terror, 1793–94

In the following month, on 27 July, Robespierre became a member of the Committee of Public Safety. This was the first political office he had held although he had clearly wielded considerable influence before this. Once on the CPS he became its spokesman and provided the main policy link with the National Convention, the Jacobin Club and the Paris Commune. So he was at the very heart of the key organs of the revolutionary government which pursued the policy of terror. His explicit responsibility was for policy on religion and, with Couthon and Saint-Just, major policy strategy and the political police. He also articulated the CPS's revolutionary theory and spoke on numerous occasions on the need for Terror. As well as linking virtue with Terror (see page 107), Robespierre also said: 'Pity is treason.' Finally he did draft the murderous Law of 22 Prairial.

Dr Marisa Linton's verdict on Robespierre

In an article 'Robespierre and the Terror' in the journal *History Today*, (August 2006), Volume 56, Issue 8 Dr Marisa Linton, Reader in History at Kingston University, gave her views on Robespierre's responsibility for the Terror. She concluded: 'The policies of the Jacobin Committees had, after all, been endorsed by the deputies of the Convention. Perhaps that is why he [Robespierre] has been so vilified: in holding one individual culpable for the ills of the Terror, French society was able to avoid looking into its own dark heart at that traumatic moment. Robespierre, you might say, took the rap.' I asked her to explain how and why she arrived at that conclusion. My questions are in red; Marisa's answers are in black.

Q **What drew you to the subject of Robespierre?**

A History for me has always been about stuff I care about. It has to be – otherwise why do it? History is written by the winners, the people who look out for their own interests, and make sure, whatever the circumstances, that they are the ones who come out on top. But I was always more interested in the losers, the people who had ideals, who tried – and usually failed – to make the world a better place. That's what drew me to Robespierre and the Jacobins. Few people failed more hopelessly than Robespierre. His efforts to bring about a 'republic of virtue' resulted in him acquiring the reputation of the leader of the Terror in the French Revolution. I was struck by Robespierre's image, that of a monster, thirsting for blood. Everyone who studies the Revolution at all knows that the Terror came to an end with the fall of Robespierre. What they often don't realise is that this was not the intention of the men who overthrew him. Robespierre wasn't killed by people who wanted to end the Terror, but by other terrorists, more violent than he was, who feared – rightly – that he was about to denounce them. Afterwards the surviving terrorists intended the Terror to continue. They were astonished when public opinion turned against the Terror. They tried to ensure that Robespierre got the sole blame for the Terror, an image that has stuck.

Q How far does Robespierre's image fit with the reality?

A Robespierre's image may be a caricature, but it is surprising how many people still believe it. The truth is more complicated and more interesting. He was a humanitarian. He started out against the death penalty which he considered to be a barbarous act. From the early more moderate days of the Revolution he was one of the most radical of the revolutionaries, a strong supporter of equal rights for poor men, for Jews, for the slaves in the French colonies. He was a man who believed in what he said. He stood out against the reckless policy that caused the French to declare war in 1792, a war that lasted till 1815, and resulted in the deaths of many millions more than those who died in the Terror. It was supposed to be a war to bring the ideals of liberty and equality to other countries, but as he rightly said 'no one welcomes armed liberators'. That war had terrible consequences, one of which was the Terror. You can't understand the Jacobins and the Terror without understanding how the experience of war and civil war affects people. The strain and fear of leading a government in such critical circumstances may lead people to take actions they would never have considered in time of peace. Robespierre did not want the war, but he was stuck with its consequences. Though he became a political leader, he had no guards, no soldiers. He didn't live in a palace, but as a lodger in the house of a master carpenter. If he really was a dictator, as his enemies said, then he made a feeble job of it.

Q Why was Robespierre overthrown, and what was the significance of this?

A For me one of the great questions about Robespierre was why he acted as he did on the day he was overthrown. When he went to the Convention that day he knew his enemies were out to get him. He faced the Convention armed with – a speech. He took no precautions to defend himself. Nothing at all. Killing Robespierre was easy. At a prearranged signal his enemies shouted him down, wouldn't let him speak, and decreed his arrest and that of his friends who tried to defend him. Within 24 hours he was dead. He had always been so astute at politics, a great survivor, over five years of turbulent revolution. Acting as he did that day was almost suicidal, as though he had finally 'lost the plot'. Why did he do it? The answer to that I think, says a lot about a man who was very genuine in his attempts to make a more humanitarian world, and who was caught up in the horror of what was actually going around him, horrors in which he had played his part, and for which he too struggled to find a meaning.

Q Are there still things we don't understand about Robespierre and Thermidor?

A It was because I was so fascinated by the French Revolution that I went to university in the first place. I have travelled a long way since then, and explored many other worlds of the past. But I keep coming back to that same problem. Why did Robespierre do it? The book I am writing now, *Choosing Terror: Virtue, Friendship, Authenticity in the French Revolution* (OUP forthcoming), is about me trying to find the answer to that question.

△ *General Bonaparte in the coup d'état of 18 Brumaire in Saint-Cloud,* painting by François Bouchot, 1840.

In 1799 General Napoleon Bonaparte, backed by the army, seized control of France in the coup of Brumaire. Within two years his position in power was secure as he was voted consul of France for life; and the Revolution was over. So what had happened between the coup of Thermidor which deposed Robespierre and this coup of Brumaire?

The men who overthrew Robespierre and his closest associates became known as the Thermidoreans. They immediately moved to end the Terror and to reverse the policy of centralisation. Within a month the Law of 22 Prairial (which had widened the definition of political crimes and made guilty verdicts far more likely – see page 109) was repealed, the Revolutionary Tribunal was reorganised and all suspects were released from prison. The power of the Committee of Public Safety was limited to just running the war and diplomacy, and its membership was to be changed more frequently. The deputies of the National Convention were now firmly back in control. They worked to produce a new constitution in 1795 and from that emerged a new revolutionary regime, the Directory. The National Convention (the legislature) was replaced by two councils, the Council of Five Hundred and the Council of Ancients, whilst the Committee of Public Safety (the executive), was replaced by the five Directors, hence the name.

In the past, as one of those 'flat spots' in history between the 'great men', Robespierre and Napoleon, this period was neglected by historians. Those who studied it tended to dismiss the Directory as corrupt and incompetent. However, rather like Weimar Germany, that may be to miss the extent to which it was a success, the line historians have taken more recently. It was after all the longest lasting revolutionary regime. Testing the degree of the Directory's success will be your enquiry in this chapter, exploring the problems that the Thermidoreans and the Directory faced, how the Directory dealt with them and just how successful it was.

The Directory

A total of thirteen men served as Directors between 1795 and 1797 but just one for the entire time. This was Paul Barras, an ex-noble and army officer responsible for the brutal suppression of counter-revolution in Marseilles and the capture of Toulon. Frightened that Robespierre was conspiring against him, he played a key role in the Thermidor coup. As a Director he gained a reputation for corruption and immorality. After the Brumaire coup Napoleon forced him out of politics and into exile.

A second Director was Lazare Carnot, ex-member of the CPS. He was spared exile at Thermidor because of his role in securing victory in the revolutionary war. He moved politically to the right and served as a Director until the coup of Fructidor (see page 120) when he fled into exile in Switzerland. He served briefly as Napoleon's War Minister but then retired into private life.

A third Director was Emmanuel Sieyès who you met back on page 41. He was elected as a Director in 1795 but refused to serve as he did not agree with the Constitution of Year III. He eventually agreed to serve from 1799 and plotted the Brumaire coup with Bonaparte. Sieyès expected to create a stronger executive that would run France more effectively but Bonaparte had other plans.

A chronology of events

Here is a timeline of the main events. These are colour coded to illustrate the difficult course the Directors (and before them the Thermidoreans) were trying to steer through that deep political divide. Those events in blue are where the Directors were in conflict with the neo-Jacobin left and drawing upon royalist support. Conversely those events in red are where the Directors were in conflict with the royalist right and drawing upon neo-Jacobin support. Those events underlined are where the army stepped in to support the government.

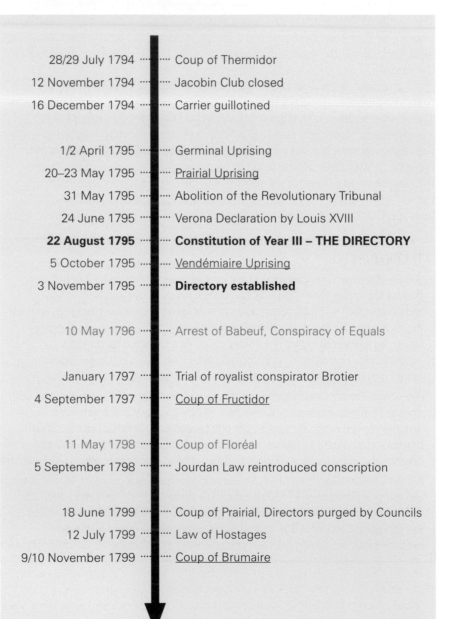

28/29 July 1794 ········· Coup of Thermidor

12 November 1794 ········· Jacobin Club closed

16 December 1794 ········· Carrier guillotined

1/2 April 1795 ········· Germinal Uprising

20–23 May 1795 ········· Prairial Uprising

31 May 1795 ········· Abolition of the Revolutionary Tribunal

24 June 1795 ········· Verona Declaration by Louis XVIII

22 August 1795 ········· **Constitution of Year III – THE DIRECTORY**

5 October 1795 ········· Vendémiaire Uprising

3 November 1795 ········· **Directory established**

10 May 1796 ········· Arrest of Babeuf, Conspiracy of Equals

January 1797 ········· Trial of royalist conspirator Brotier

4 September 1797 ········· Coup of Fructidor

11 May 1798 ········· Coup of Floréal

5 September 1798 ········· Jourdan Law reintroduced conscription

18 June 1799 ········· Coup of Prairial, Directors purged by Councils

12 July 1799 ········· Law of Hostages

9/10 November 1799 ········· Coup of Brumaire

■ Enquiry Focus: How successful was the Directory?

1 To help you gather evidence for this enquiry construct a table like the one below and complete it as you read this chapter. In the left-hand column enter the seven problems faced by the Directory:
   - the economy, notably inflation
   - government finance
   - political violence
   - deep political divisions
   - internal revolt
   - foreign war
   - weaknesses of the 1795 constitution.

2 In the final column note any implications of the Directory's policies. Did they make the Directory popular or unpopular; decrease public confidence in the constitution of 1795; make the Directory more dependent upon army support to survive?

Problem	Directory's response	Outcome of response – benefits or drawbacks	Judgement success or failure	Future implications of Directory policies
The economy				

The economy

The economic problems the Directory faced were the same as those of previous regimes – inflation, a valueless currency and high food prices. In 1795 the Thermidoreans had abolished the Maximum (a set of price fixing regulations) to move back to a free market. This led to rampant inflation which destroyed the purchasing power of the *assignat*, the revolutionary paper currency. Added to this was a very hard winter. Together these led to great increases in the price of bread and this prompted two protests in Paris. The first on 12–13 Germinal (1–2 April) was a mass demonstration at the National Convention which the National Guards dispersed without violence. The second on 1–4 Prairial (20–23 May) was a more serious rising with both sides armed but was eventually dealt with by the army.

By the start of the Directory the value of the *assignat* had plummeted to one per cent of its face value. Two anecdotes illustrate the depth of the problem – firstly the story of the floor of the *assignat* printing press collapsing under the weight of new *assignats* being printed and secondly the salaries to be paid to the Directors were expressed not in *assignats* but in kind, in grain. In an attempt to solve inflation the Directory tried introducing a new paper currency. This experiment lasted just over a year and was a complete failure. The paper currency was withdrawn and so from February 1787 metal coins were the only legal currency. As there were not enough coins in circulation this hampered commerce and deflation resulted. The Directory thus never satisfactorily solved the economic problem or passed **lasting reforms**, and in failing made itself unpopular with people at all social levels.

One **lasting reform** was the introduction of the metric system of weights and measures on 18 Germinal III (7 April 1795). The research into this had been commissioned by Louis XVI and the National Assembly in order to give France a unified and rational system of weights and measures to replace all the regional variations of Ancien Régime France.

Government finance

With government finances, the Directory was more successful in balancing the books. In September 1797 two thirds of the national debt was written off through the issue of bonds to government creditors. These bonds could be used to buy national property, in other words property taken from the crown, the Church and others. However, these bonds fell in value and became worthless. In effect the government had gone bankrupt and it was known at the time as the 'bankruptcy of two thirds'. So although the debt was greatly reduced, which in turn reduced the interest payments, the original government creditors were alienated. The Directory would not be able to rely upon their future support.

For government income, the Directory in part relied upon the profits of war, plunder taken from those parts of Germany and Italy occupied by French armies. For example, on 15 May 1796 Bonaparte made the city of Milan pay a huge ransom. This had the benefit of enabling the Directory to function but had the drawback of making it more reliant on the army and on an aggressive war policy.

A more lasting solution was provided by the Finance Minister, Vincent Ramel. In 1798 he reformed the tax system introducing four new direct taxes, most notably the tax on doors and windows which hit the rich hardest. He also reintroduced an Ancien Régime indirect tax, the *octrois*, a tax on goods brought into towns which was very unpopular. And he made tax collection more efficient. The benefit of this was that by 1798 the government finances balanced. But the drawbacks were that it lost support for the Directory from those adversely affected by the bankruptcy and by the new taxes; and the policy of making war for plunder increased its reliance on the army.

Political violence

The Thermidoreans were keen to distance themselves from the Jacobin terror although many were themselves Jacobins. This led them to shift the blame for the Terror on to Robespierre and his closest associates, many of whom had died with him. Of the worst surviving terrorists Jean-Baptiste Carrier was guillotined in 1794 whilst after the Germinal rising Barère, Billaud-Varenne and Collot d'Herbois were exiled to Guiana, the '**dry guillotine**'.

After Thermidor, in the streets of Paris the *jeunesse dorée* (literally gilded youth who were organised gangs of young men) went around attacking *sans-culottes*, former militants and Jacobins. Their stoning of the Jacobin Club was used as a pretext for it to be closed down. Meanwhile, in the south of France, in Lyons and the Rhone valley where the Terror had been so brutal there were equally savage reprisals by those who had been affected, including prison massacres and street killings. At least 2000 died in this '**White Terror**' in 1795 and it continued into the years that followed. When the Directory came into power, it too struggled to control the violence which remained widespread in the countryside throughout the period. When local juries failed to convict, the Directory divided France into military districts, set up military commissions to judge cases and employed army generals to maintain law and order. But even this undemocratic approach did not fully work. The Directory failed to completely solve the problem of lawlessness and disorder.

■ Complete your table and make your judgement on the Directory's handling of the **economy** and of **government finance**.

dry guillotine
Deportation to Guiana was known as the 'dry guillotine' as the climate killed so many

White Terror
This was the targeted killing of *sans-culotte* militants, members of surveillance committees who had denounced suspects and other former Jacobin officials. The killings were done by secret murder gangs

Political divisions

France was deeply divided not just by a desire for revenge but also by deep political differences. On the left the *sans-culottes* were finished as a political force by the failure of their uprisings and the military suppression and executions that followed. The Directory could not use them to stay in power as the Jacobin dictatorship had. Moreover it was from the extreme left that the first real threat to the Directory came with the Babeuf Plot in 1796. In his 'conspiracy of equals' Gracchus Babeuf planned to organise a small group of revolutionaries who would persuade the police and the army to help them seize power. He intended to set up a dictatorship to make France a radically different society with ideas some historians view as an early form of communism. His plot failed and he went to the guillotine.

Despite the White Terror and the closure of their power base, the Jacobin Club, the **neo-Jacobins** remained a powerful political force. In the coup of Floréal in 1798 the Directory arranged to annul the election of 127 deputies, many of whom were suspected of being neo-Jacobins. They were successful in doing this and so headed off a possible neo-Jacobin challenge to their policies. However, in breaking the constitution the Directors undermined its public standing, and ultimately their own legitimacy as a government. Later in 1799 when the neo-Jacobins were in control of the Councils the Law of Hostages was passed. Under this law resistance to any new or existing laws could lead to an area being declared disturbed. Then the relatives of nobles or *émigrés* could be arrested, fined and imprisoned for any damage done by those causing the disturbance.

> **Neo-Jacobins** or new Jacobins

The royalists had benefited from political amnesties which released those royalists still in prison after Thermidor, and some of the *émigrés* and non-swearing clergy took the opportunity to return home. The royalists however were split. On one hand there were those who wanted a return to the Ancien Régime and on the other hand those who only wanted to turn the clock back to 1791 and a constitutional monarchy. When little Louis XVII died alone in his prison cell in June 1795 his uncle, the Comte de Provence, claimed the throne and issued the Verona Declaration promising to restore the ancient constitution, to restore all properties 'stolen' from the Church and from the *émigrés* and to execute the regicides. In the same month there was an *émigré* landing, complete with their own guillotine to execute revolutionaries, made with British assistance at Quiberon Bay. This was defeated and a second *émigré* landing at Ile de Yeu off the Vendée also failed.

In this climate the deputies of the National Convention passed the 'Law of two thirds'. This ensured that the new Councils would be dominated by men committed to the continuation of the Revolution. This prompted the Vendémiaire uprising in Paris. A crowd estimated at as many as 25,000 tried to surround the National Convention but it was dispersed by a much smaller army force, which crucially used Napoleon's cannon fire. This is usually described as a royalist uprising but it had economic origins too.

Just like the neo-Jacobins the constitutional monarchists remained a powerful political force during the Directory even though their efforts were sometimes hampered by the extremists. For example, in January 1797 when André Brotier, a royalist agent, and his fellow conspirators were arrested for planning to persuade troops in Paris to overthrow the government (like Babeuf had before them).

■ Complete your table and make your judgement on the Directory's handling of **political violence** and **political divisions**. You may want to divide the latter section into two parts to cover threats from the left and right of the political spectrum.

In 1797 the royalists did very well in the elections. They were able to put their supporters into important positions including the Presidents of the Councils, and two of the Directors were sympathisers. This prompted the remaining three Directors to seek the help of the army. In the coup of Fructidor soldiers took control of Paris, surrounded the Councils' meeting places and arrested 53 deputies and two Directors. The remaining deputies were then intimidated into cancelling elections in many areas, removing 177 deputies and leaving many areas unrepresented. In a second decree the arrested deputies, Directors and other leading royalists were sent to Guiana. So the Directory had stayed in control but at the expense of undermining the status of the constitution and by relying upon the army. In the aftermath there was a limited Directorial Terror. *Émigrés* were given two weeks to leave France or face execution as were the non-swearing clergy. This led to 160 death sentences. This expulsion of clergy served also to turn Catholics against the Directory.

Internal revolt

As well as dealing with political violence the Directory had to cope with internal revolt in Brittany, and later Normandy, where a movement known as the Chouans emerged. They were based in the countryside and unlike the earlier revolt in the Vendée never actually held any territory. Instead the Chouans fought a guerrilla war attacking small groups of troops and killing local officials. Historians see it as a largely peasant movement, with some aristocratic involvement. As well as seeing the Revolution as threatening their religion, royalism appears to have been more of a motivating factor for the rebels. When the *émigrés* landed at Quiberon Bay they were joined by thousands of Chouans. After that defeat the Chouans reverted to their guerrilla tactics. Taking decisive action the Directory provided General Hoche with a large army to suppress the revolt in Brittany, and the Vendée where fighting had broken out again. By 1796 he had restored peace and order to western France. This was undone in September 1798 when the Jourdan Law reintroduced conscription. Chounanism in opposition to this broke out again.

War

When the Directory came to power there were no foreign armies on French soil so successful had the army been since Fleurus. By 1796 France only faced Britain and Austria. The other members of the First Coalition had been knocked out of the war and two of them, the Spanish and the Dutch had become France's allies. The Directory's aim in 1796 was to defeat Austria and this was achieved, partly due to a brilliant Italian campaign by Bonaparte. That left just Britain but an invasion was made impossible by British naval victories over the Spanish and Dutch fleets.

The Directory now began to follow a more aggressive policy of conquest, and then the setting up new republican states especially in Italy. There were a number of reasons for this war policy.

- The first was that war became essential to the Directory's survival. Money from Italy staved off bankruptcy in 1797. Defeated states were required to pay **indemnities**. Those in Germany paid 16 million *livres* whilst those in Italy paid in the region of 200 million.

- Secondly, war kept the army happy and **ambitious generals** occupied, so doubly ensuring the Directory's survival.

- Thirdly, there was an element of corruption. Under the Jacobin dictatorship the state controlled the supply of the armies but under the Directory this was done by private contractors, some of whom made vast fortunes and acquired political influence through their friendships with Directors. There was undoubtedly a link between the Directory and war profiteering.

indemnities
An indemnity is a sum of money paid in compensation by a country defeated in war to the winning country

In 1797 the Directory over reached itself. Bonaparte set off with his army to attack British interests in Egypt. Whilst his military campaign was very successful, he and his army were trapped in Egypt when the French fleet that took them there was destroyed by the British fleet led by Nelson. Meanwhile this aggressive action had antagonised other European powers and a Second Coalition was formed against France. In 1799 French forces were defeated by the Prussians and Austrians and to a French population already weary of a war that had begun back in 1791 this increased the unpopularity of the Directory.

The danger of **ambitious generals** trying to seize power for themselves is a thread running through the Revolution from Lafayette to Bonaparte.

> ■ Complete your table and make your judgement on the Directory's handling of the **internal revolt** and **foreign war**.

The War of the Second Coalition 1799–1802

In 1799 France's apparent military weakness coupled with the continuing hostility of the other European powers led to the outbreak of war again. The Austrians and Russians formed a new alliance and attempted to reverse France's previous military conquests in Germany and Italy. Initially the French were driven back on all fronts but the tide had turned by 1800. Russia dropped out after military defeats and over Britain's insistence on searching shipping in the Baltic. Meanwhile the French armies under Napoleon defeated the Austrians in Italy at the battle of Marengo (14 June 1800) whilst north of the Alps General Moreau defeated the Austrians at the battle of Hohenlinden (3 December 1800). Austria then made peace leaving just Britain to continue the war at sea until the Treaty of Amiens in 1802 ended hostilities.

Weaknesses of the 1795 constitution

The 1795 constitution on which the Directory was based was a democracy of sorts. The **franchise** was based upon a tax threshold but even so 5.5 out of 8 million adult males were entitled to vote. The constitution also provided for annual elections with numbers of deputies being required to seek re-election. So until Fructidor 1797 it could be claimed that the Directory successfully provided a moderate democratic government, steering a middle way between a reintroduction of the monarchy on the right and the introduction of a popular democracy on the left. In doing so it demonstrated that democracy could work.

franchise
The right to vote

■ Complete your table and make your judgement on the Directory's handling of the **constitution**.

However, within the constitution there were a number of inherent weaknesses. The annual elections led to instability. More seriously there was no mechanism to resolve the situation when the executive, the Directors, disagreed with the legislature, the Councils. It could be argued that this was the reason for the Directors increasing disregard of the Constitution as they tried to maintain control of the Councils. This policy led to a general fall in confidence in the constitution and one indicator of that was the declining turn out of voters in elections over the period.

■ Concluding your enquiry

Your completed table should show you that in some respects the Directory was a success. Certainly it initiated a number of measures which later regimes could build upon, such as the introduction of the first central schools, one per department, which replaced the old church-run schools and would form the basis of later steps towards a national system of state run education. Then there was the metric system (see page 117) and the ground work for the setting up of the French National Bank which was so important to later financial stability. However, this is balanced by its failures.

1 What is your final judgment on the Directory? Write a short assessment which identifies the balance of success and failure.

2 The other enquiry question that we could have considered is 'Why did the Directory fall? Here your **future implications** column should provide you with an answer.

Napoleon Bonaparte (1769–1821)

Napoleon was born in Ajaccio, Corsica in 1769, just one year after it joined France. The son of a minor aristocratic family he was sent to France for his education and entered the École Militaire in Paris in 1784. He trained as an artillery officer and was its first Corsican graduate. He was commissioned as a second lieutenant and but for the Revolution might have had a modest career. However, after 1789 he was able to take advantage of the increased opportunities for promotion for able officers. He was in favour of the Revolution and wrote a pro-revolutionary pamphlet which brought him to the attention of Robespierre's younger brother, Augustin.

His first military achievement of note was when as commander of the artillery at the siege of Toulon he devised the plan which drove the British navy out. This won him promotion to brigadier general in charge of the artillery of the army of Italy. After Thermidor his association with Robespierre led to him being imprisoned briefly. A number of military commands followed but his career looked to be blocked when he refused to serve against the Vendean rebels. However, in 1795 he was in Paris, in the right place at the right time. Placed in charge of the temporary forces assembled to defend the National Convention against the Vendémiaire uprising his use of cannon fire was crucial. This earned him promotion and command of the army of Italy.

◁ *Napoleon Crossing the Saint Bernard,* painted in 1800 by Jacques-Louis David. In reality Napoleon crossed the Alps on a mule, not a horse.

In 1796–97 Napoleon fought a very successful campaign in Italy collecting a great deal of money which helped finance the Directory. He sent back troops to help the Directory in the coup of Fructidor. After finally defeating the Austrians he negotiated the advantageous Treaty of Campo Formio without consulting the Directory and returned to France a hero.

In 1799 he returned to France from his Egyptian campaign as news had reached him of the French defeats by the forces of the Second Coalition. Back in France the full scale of the failure in Egypt was not known and he was still received as a hero. Again he was in the right place at the right time. Sieyès, the chief plotter of the coup of Brumaire, intended to change the constitution of 1795 which he had never approved of. He needed military support for this and, as his favoured candidate General Joubert had been killed in Italy, he turned to Napoleon. Napoleon however had other ideas and out manoeuvred Sieyès to seize power for himself as First Consul. Napoleon's position as undisputed ruler of France was consolidated in 1802 when he was voted Consul for life, when the Revolutionary Wars were brought to an end by the Peace of Amiens and when his **Concordat** with the Pope went some way towards healing the divisions between the State and the Church.

In the **Concordat** the Catholic Church recognised the Revolution and agreed not to try and recover Church lands. The French Church was to remain under state control with clergy paid and appointed by the government and the Catholic faith could be practiced in France, although other religions were also to be tolerated.

10 Did all revolutionaries share Robespierre's motives?

On the 10 Thermidor Year II (28 July 1794) Robespierre mounted the steps of the scaffold in the Place de la Revolution. He had spent the previous night in custody and in great pain from the pistol shot that had shattered his jaw. That morning he and his close colleagues had been taken before the Revolutionary Tribunal and identified. As rebels that was all that was required to secure their death sentences. Now it was early evening. On the scaffold the executioners took off his sky blue coat. His biographer Ruth Scurr takes up the story.

> Just before they strapped him to the plank, they decided to rip off the bandage that was holding his face together. Perhaps the executioner – so experienced by now – thought the bandage was thick enough to get in the way of the descending blade; perhaps he wanted to be cruel. Robespierre screamed. It was the deep, sharp cry of a man in excruciating pain that you hear sometimes in hospitals – the violent protest of a wounded human animal that, however brave or bent on self-control, cannot stop the voice of torment. Anyone who has ever heard a man scream knows how Robespierre sounded then.
>
> The scream was the last act of the man who had tried as no one else did to embody the Revolution. It was the point of severance, when Robespierre's precious vision of a democratic republic, pure and founded on virtue, finally left him.

■ Enquiry Focus: Did all revolutionaries share Robespierre's motives?

Since his death, all of Robespierre's writings and speeches have been collected and published and serve as a valuable archive for historians. I find myself in agreement with those historians like Ruth Scurr and Marisa Linton who view Robespierre as a man motivated by his idealism. But what motivated so many other French men and women to support the Revolution, knowing that in doing so they risked losing their lands, their career, their freedom, their friends, their wives and ultimately their lives?

Were they also motivated by idealism or did they have other motives? Was their motive the pursuit of power and the wealth that power could bring? Was it out of resentment towards the old regime and its injustices? Was it a career choice or simply a matter of survival?

In the following pages you will find the roles of a number of individuals described and their possible motives discussed. Your task is to decide whether they shared Robespierre's idealism or had other motives. It is up to you how you record your conclusions.

You may notice that some information in this section is repeated from earlier in the book. This has been done deliberately to speed up your completion of the enquiry.

Philippe, Duc D'Orleans (1747–93), later known as Philippe Égalité

Philippe, Duc D'Orleans was Louis XVI's cousin, a member of the Bourbon royal family and a Prince of the Blood. He was also married to the richest woman in France. Until the 1770s he lived a debauched and frivolous life but then became involved in politics. He embraced the ideas of the Enlightenment and argued for reform. At the Assembly of Notables in 1787 and in the Paris Parlement he criticised the government. For this he was exiled by *lettre de cachet*. Already an enemy of Marie Antoinette, this placed Orleans in opposition to Louis XVI as well. To some he was an idealist in favour of reform but others suspected his motives. They saw Orleans as aiming for the crown himself, an accusation he always denied.

As you have seen on page 17 one place where revolutionary ideas spread were the masonic lodges and Orleans had become Grand Master of the French Masonic order back in 1771. By 1789 his Paris home, the Palais-Royal, was a base for the patriot party. He funded and protected the journalists and agitators who attacked Louis' government. Their pamphlets could be published uncensored at the Palais-Royal and it was perhaps no accident that the starting point of the attack on the Bastille was the Café Foy within its grounds.

△ *The Duc D'Orleans*, an engraved portrait by Philbert Debucourt 1789.

Orleans was certainly committed to the Revolution. In 1789 he was elected as a Second Estate deputy to the Estates-General, and led the first group of nobles to break ranks and join the National Assembly. This earned him the hatred of his fellow nobles as a class traitor. He was suspected and, later, found to be behind the October Days, the march on Versailles in 1789 which nearly resulted in the death of Marie Antoinette. The upheaval that followed may have been the chance to seize the throne he was looking for, but if it was he missed it.

Whilst other aristocrats fled abroad Orleans remained in Paris. He was a member of the Jacobin Club and in 1793, as a member of the National Convention, he voted for the death of Louis XVI. He even changed his name to Phillipe Égalité but this was not enough to save him during the Terror. When his soldier son, the future King Louis-Philippe I, defected to the Austrians in April 1793 Orleans was arrested. On the 6 November 1793 he was tried, convicted and executed.

Benjamin Franklin who knew him wrote:

> Yes, he has some faults but all are outweighed by his many virtues that he has displayed in these difficult times. He has true character, original if eccentric, but he is driven by a desire for vengeance against oppression and the need to attain freedom for himself and his people.

Tom Ambrose titled his 2008 biography *Godfather of the Revolution: The Life of Philippe Égalité, Duc D'Orleans*.

■ Which motives may have driven Orleans (perhaps idealism? power?) and why might it be difficult to decide on which dominated his thinking?

Jacques-Louis David (1748–1825) 'Citizen Artist'

While Philippe, Duc D'Orleans came from the top rank of French society, Jacques-Louis David came from humbler beginnings. He was born in Paris and when his tradesman father died young his mother's wealthy relatives provided him with an expensive education. David became a student in the Paris studio of the artist Joseph-Marie Vien and, after winning the Prix de Rome competition, went to Rome to continue his artistic studies.

He came home in 1780 and exhibited his work with huge success in the Salons of 1781 and 1783. But at the same time he came into conflict with authority, the Royal Academy. This was the government agency which had strict rules about art, rules David would not conform to. In 1784, now one of France's leading artists, he returned to Rome to work on the *Oath of the Horatii* (1785) accompanied by 40 students. Back again in Paris he exhibited it to great acclaim in the Salon of 1785. His paintings of classical republican Roman subjects emphasised such ideas as patriotism and the sacrifice of the individual to the state, and this fitted with the current intellectual climate. By 1789, whilst his aristocratic patrons included the King's brother, he was being seen as the artist whose work best captured the ideals of the Revolution.

David's personal artistic struggle with the Royal Academy evolved into a political one with him leading those artists who were anxious to make the Royal Academy more democratic. David appealed to the National Assembly for support and from here on his involvement in the Revolution increased. As its recorder, he planned the *Tennis Court Oath* painting, April 1789, before having to abandon it. A second, more controversial, project *Louis XVI Showing the Constitution to his son* also had to be abandoned in 1792. Both paintings were overtaken by events. David denied he had ever started painting the King, but the surviving preliminary sketches prove otherwise.

David joined the Jacobin Club in 1790 and stayed when the constitutional monarchists left. He moved politically left as the Revolution did. He actively supported his friends Marat and Robespierre and was elected to the National Convention in September 1792. As well as a participant he became a designer and propagandist for the Revolution. The historian Simon Schama describes him as a 'citizen artist'. David organised the ten great festivals of the Revolution. He also designed uniforms, banners, triumphal arches, and inspirational props. This left him less time for painting, but he did complete two famous martyr paintings *Lepelletier* (1793) and *Marat breathing his last* (1793).

For the *Tennis Court Oath* see page 50 and for *Marat breathing his last* see page 93.

He became a willing and active member of the Jacobin leadership. He served a term as president of the National Convention in January 1794 and as president of the Jacobin Club. He was a member of the Committee of General Security from September 1793 and signed over 400 of its decrees, many of which were for the arrest of suspects. One historian reports David's signature on the execution orders of more than 300 people, although this was only ten per cent of those issued. Certainly as a deputy of the National Convention, David voted for the deaths of both the King and Marie Antoinette. When he did this his wife divorced him.

When Robespierre was overthrown in the coup of Thermidor David was not present in the National Convention. If he had been he might have been guillotined too. He later said that he had been unwell. As it was, he was arrested a few days later. Charged with being a supporter of Robespierre he survived two spells of imprisonment during 1794 and 1795. In prison David wrote many letters in his own defence. In one to a student he wrote: 'I am prevented from returning to my studio, which, alas, I should never have left. I believed that in accepting the most honourable position, but very difficult to fill, that of legislator, that a righteous heart would suffice, but I lacked the second quality, understanding.' He painted more eloquently than he wrote!

Eventually released David went back to his painting, and remarried his wife. In 1797 he met Napoleon. Napoleon saw David's value as a propagandist and sat for a portrait. The one and only sitting lasted for three hours, and the resultant *Portrait of Bonaparte* was never finished. But David went on to become the official painter of the Napoleonic regime. When Napoleon fell from power in 1815 David, as a regicide, went into exile. He lived the remainder of his life in Brussels refusing to return to a France ruled by a king. But he remained a patriot. Invited by the Duke of Wellington to paint his portrait David wrote: 'I have not waited 70 years to defile my brush. I would rather cut off my hand than paint an Englishman.'

△ *Self Portrait*, oil on canvas, 81x64 cm. David painted this whilst in prison in the Hotel des Fermes in 1794. He deliberately depicted himself as a young idealist as part of his defence against charges of Terrorism. Here he appears much younger than in an earlier self portrait of 1791. Does this lessen the usefulness of his art as source material for us as historians of the Revolution?

David's life encapsulates the course of the Revolution. He began as a client of the Ancien Régime and moved to oppose it; next he moved from revolutionary idealist and propagandist to regicide and terrorist; then he moved from prisoner to Napoleonic propagandist and finally he died in exile while a new Bourbon king reigned.

As the official painter David's paintings from this time include: *Napoleon Crossing the Saint-Bernard* (1801) (see page 123) and *Coronation of Napoleon and Josephine in Notre Dame* (1806).

■ Was idealism the driving force behind David's support for the Revolution, or was he motivated by resentment of authority or by friendship or by a mixture of all three?

Georges Jacques Danton (1759–94)

Unlike Robespierre there is little reliable evidence about Danton as he left few letters or written speeches. Certainly he was ambitious. Before the Revolution he sometimes used the aristocratic form of his name, D'Anton. Equally certainly he was influenced by Enlightenment ideas and by Roman republican ideas. It was said he could recite the Roman republican philosopher Cicero's speeches from memory. As a speaker he came to political prominence in the Cordeliers district and club in 1789 and later in the Jacobin Club.

In the aftermath of the Massacre of the Champs de Mars (July 1791), Danton, one of the organisers of the republican petition, fled to England to avoid arrest. When he returned that autumn he was elected deputy *procureur* of Paris. From this important post he increased his power base in the city. Unlike Robespierre, Danton was quite happy to accept office and make money from it.

△ *Danton*, graphite sketch c. 1793 by Jacques-Louis David.

As the revolutionary seen to speak for the *sans-culottes* he was possibly the key figure in the final overthrow of the monarchy in August 1792. Immediately afterwards Danton was appointed Minister of Justice in the provisional government that controlled France until October. In that time he did not prevent the September Massacres but did crucially rally support for the war effort.

He was elected to the National Convention where he sat in 'the Mountain'. There he was attacked by the Girondins who hated him for his complicity in the September Massacres and who accused him of corruption. He voted for the death of Louis XVI and was instrumental in the setting up of the apparatus of the Terror, that is the Revolutionary Tribunal and the Committee of Public Safety of which he was one of the original nine members. He said, '… let us be terrible, to dispense the people from the need to be terrible themselves'.

In the later stages of the Terror, following illness and a spell at home, Danton returned to Paris and campaigned to bring the Terror to an end. Back in Paris he lost the power struggle with Robespierre and was arrested, tried and executed. His last words to the executioner were: 'Don't forget to show my head to the people. It's well worth seeing.'

David Lawday titled his 2009 biography *Danton: Gentle Giant of Terror*.

■ Did Danton share Robespierre's idealism or was he motivated by power and the wealth it brought, or was it a mixture of both? Why might identifying Danton's motives be particularly difficult?

Madame Roland (1754–93)

Marie-Jean Phlipon, better known as Madame Roland, was born in Paris. The only surviving daughter of a middle-class engraver she was tutored at home and was heavily influenced by the classical writer Plutarch and the Enlightenment authors, Montesquieu, Voltaire and Rousseau. She wrote, 'I had hated kings since I was a child and I could never witness without an involuntary shudder the spectacle of a man abasing himself before another man.'

In 1781 she married Jean-Marie Roland, 20 years her elder, and moved to Lyons. They were supporters of the Revolution from the beginning and contributed to Brissot's revolutionary newspaper, the *Patriote français*. When Roland himself came to political prominence in Paris in 1791 she was able to exert considerable influence on the course of the Revolution, both through him and through her salon at the Hotel Britannique. Many of the leading revolutionary figures attended her salon, including Brissot and Robespierre. The men discussed events and agreed on strategy for influencing both the Jacobin Club and the National Assembly. Unlike other political hostesses, she chose not to be the centre of attention and did not speak until the meetings ended. No women were invited.

△ Madam Roland portrait painted c.1787 by Adélaide Labille-Guiard.

In March 1792, Louis XVI appointed a new cabinet which included many Girondin ministers, Roland being one. Madame Roland was often present when colleagues and friends brought up matters of state with her husband at home. She provided advice and support for his policies and wrote much of his correspondence. This placed her at the social and political centre of the Girondin government. Robespierre for one was hostile to what he saw as a return to the Ancien Régime style of doing government.

When the Jacobins split in early 1792 the Rolands were firmly identified with the Girondin faction. She particularly hated Danton both for his alleged corruption and for his part in the September Massacres. Of these she wrote in a letter to a political ally: 'You know my passion for the Revolution. Well, I am ashamed of it! It has been ruined by scoundrels. It has turned hideous.'

When the Girondins lost the political struggle with the Montagnards and were themselves purged and arrested she organised her husband's escape but was herself arrested on the 1 June 1793. After five months in prison she was tried on the charge of having royalist sympathies, and convicted. She went to the guillotine on 8 November 1793. Her last words on the scaffold as she saw David's statue of Liberty were reportedly, 'Oh Liberty, what crimes are committed in thy name'. When he heard the news of her death her husband came out of hiding and committed suicide, impaling himself on his sword stick.

■ Was Madame Roland motivated by idealism? Do her motives appear to have changed over time or was it the Revolution that changed?

Sans-culottes, the individuals in the crowd

You have met the *sans-culottes* a number of times in this book and will be aware that they were the small property owners and artisans active in Parisian sectional politics. Marxist historians like Georges Rudé have argued that they were a definable social group while more recently, revisionist historians such as Richard Andrews have seen the *sans-culottes* not as a social class but as a political grouping. But both see the *sans-culottes* as the leaders who could bring out onto the streets the Parisian masses, the crowd, as political muscle. For Rudé the motivation of the crowd was quite straight forward, 'the primary and most constant motive impelling revolutionary crowds during this period was the concern for the cheap and plentiful food'. He pointed to the troubles that broke out in the queues outside bakers towards the end of the Ancien Régime, government measures to try and keep control by stationing troops in markets and guards at bakers' doors and the popular fears that the government was deliberately trying to starve the people of Paris.

Fear and rumour was a powerful factor in some of the early major events of the Revolution such as the fears that Louis' government was planning to use force which prompted the raids on gun shops, the storming of the Invalides in search of weapons and finally the storming of the Bastille in July 1789. Another example is the fear that counter-revolutionaries would help the Prussians to capture Paris that prompted the September Massacres of 1792.

But if the motivation of the crowd can be generalised, the motivation of the *sans-culottes* cannot. Andrews argues that the *sans-culottes* cannot be seen as a single, unchanging social grouping but instead was composed of shifting and competing groups in each of the 48 sections of Paris. He has used the available records to study in detail these men whom he describes as having chosen the '*sans-culotte*' career and its vocation of power. For him the divisions between them were personal and political.

One *sans-culotte* who might illustrate the pursuit of power argument was Aristarque Didot. Didot was the son of a well off provincial magistrate and part of a wealthy publishing family who employed roughly 250 people in their print works and bookshops in Paris and who also owned paper mills at Essonne. Aged 25 he served as a revolutionary commissioner in the Reunion section in 1793 and was viewed as strict in his application of the Law of Suspects. He drafted a resolution against the hoarding of food and called for the regulation of trade in vital commodities. In November 1793 a pamphlet of his was published that blamed the troubles of the French republic on the attacks of foreign monarchs, betrayals by ministers and generals, and the greed and ill will of merchants and the rich. He was imprisoned as a suspected **Hébertist** in February 1794 and again in May 1795, this time as a terrorist. However, by January 1796 he was free and serving as a clerk in the Ministry of General Police and by 1797 he was a principal clerk. Like many others the revolutionary state had given him an opportunity to 'get on' in life.

Another *sans-culotte* Andrews has focused upon was Jean-Charles Chemin from the Pont Neuf section. Chemin was imprisoned on 21 March 1794, also as a suspected Hébertist. He was an affluent haberdashery and hosiery merchant, aged in his 50s, and one of the leaders in his section. In a petition for his release sent to the Committees of General Security and Public Safety 75 of his fellow citizens described his revolutionary contributions:

Hébertists were a loose coalition around the journalist Hébert who formed an opposition to the revolutionary government in 1793–94 who called for higher taxes on the rich, death for hoarders and the arrest of political suspects, in short more terror.

Ardently, he declared for liberty from its very dawning; on 14 July, 1789 he raced to the Invalides Arsenal to gather weapons, he participated in the festival of Chateau-Vieux, in the insurrections of 10 August and 31 May, and in all the events of the Revolution … He regularly attends the popular societies … He has always been of patriotic principles, but since his love for the Revolution could have degenerated into fanaticism (if one may use that word); because he possess only the most common measure of intellect and no education, he could have committed errors with the purest of intentions.

From prison he wrote to the Committees of Government on his motives.

I proclaim, and I call upon all patriots who know me to attest that since 1789 all of my time has been absolutely devoted to public service; I have figured in all the days of the Revolution … I sent one of my sons to the Vendée, where he died on the field of battle, …

Finally as an example that the *sans-culottes* were not a single class but instead were competing elites in each section struggling for control, Andrews points to two men, Guillaume Desmonceaux and Francois-Pierre Beaudouin, enemies in the Gravilliers section. Both men were of a similar age and both were decorative building painters who owned property and employed six or seven highly skilled workers. But that did not stop the latter from imprisoning the former for his constitutional monarchy sympathies; and if the Feuillants had been successful in maintaining a constitutional monarchy then no doubt it would have been Beaudouin who would have been imprisoned for his republican sympathies.

■ What range of motives influenced the *sans-culottes*? Why is it difficult to identify single motives for any individual?

▽ A *Sans-culotte* with His Pike, a Carter, a Market Porter, a Cobbler and a Carpenter, a Giclee patriotic print by the Le Sueur Brothers.

François de Neufchâteau (1750–1828)

François de Neufchâteau was the son of a school teacher who after marrying for money bought an administrative office and so entered the service of Louis XVI's government. As well as an administrator he was also a poet, playwright and translator. Neufchâteau served as a magistrate in Lorraine before, in 1783, he was appointed *procureur-général* to the council of the French colony of Saint Domingue in the Caribbean. It was while serving in this position that he came to see and articulate his purpose in life as doing good. In this particular case that meant improving conditions for the colonists and in order to do so he moved from simply enforcing royal authority to actually taking on some of it for himself. The historian James Livesey comments that:

> François de Neufchâteau was effectively practising revolution as a career, acting as a citizen rather than as the representative of the King, even before the Revolution had begun.

Livesey sees the idea of practising revolution as a career as emerging during the Enlightenment. It was a development from the religious idea of a vocation or calling. For Neufchâteau, and men like him, this notion of a career combined three things – his own self-interest, his political role and his moral duty to do good. And to achieve this, men had to work under the laws they made themselves, an idea that can be linked to Rousseau's thinking. And so it was this that allowed men like Neufchâteau to evolve from a loyal servant of the crown to a republican revolutionary.

In 1791 Neufchâteau was elected to the Legislative Assembly and was an active deputy. He was later elected to the National Convention but refused to serve. He fell foul of the Committee of Public Safety who felt royalist views were being expressed in his play *Pamela* which was performed on the 1 August 1793. Neufchâteau and the cast were imprisoned but he survived the Terror. He later wrote that on 10 Thermidor (28 July 1794): 'the famous David met me on the staircase of the prison and said to me smiling "Ah! Robespierre forgot about you."'

Neufchâteau went on to serve as an administrator in Lorraine after the coup of Thermidor, became Minister of the Interior in 1797 and served as a Director until Brumaire. Under Napoleon he continued to serve as an administrator and encouraged economic growth and technological and educational innovation until he retired from public life with the Bourbon restoration in 1814.

> ■ It sounds as if Neufchâteau was driven by his career – but was this as selfish as it sounds or were there other motives behind his pursuit of his career?

Conclusions – exploring motivations

Some of the individuals we have looked at in this chapter survived the Revolution whilst others did not. In risking their lives in such a turbulent period we can see that some were motivated by idealism whilst others sought power or simply to stay alive. But it is difficult to give a definitive answer to the question 'What motivated the revolutionaries?' We have identified a range of motives but it is very difficult to be certain about which ones dominated each individual's thinking at any point in time. So why is it so difficult?

a) Accounts written by others are of limited value as they couldn't see into another person's mind.

b) Individuals may have left very little written evidence behind, (as with Danton who wrote few letters).

c) Their own explanations have to be questioned because they needed to present the explanation most likely to win public support or to secure their own safety. For example, Robespierre's copious papers are those of a polished politician whilst the memoires of Madame Roland, written in prison whilst awaiting her execution, were penned to defend her reputation as a citizen of the republic who stayed true to the ideals of Rousseau and Voltaire.

d) Motives change over time. In a period of such dramatic events as the calling of the Estates-General, the storming of the Bastille, the overthrow of the monarchy, people's motives change. Think of how individuals moved from one political club to another, such as from the Jacobins to the Feuillants. We all know from our own experience when making up our minds about something complicated that different factors jostle for dominance in our minds and swap around in significance.

e) We don't know whether people were thinking rationally throughout or whether they were suffering from depression, as is suggested of Louis in 1789, or from a mental breakdown as is suggested for Robespierre in 1794. People may sometimes panic and take a bad decision as perhaps Lafayette did in attempting to turn his army on Paris and then in defecting to the Austrians.

f) Finally, there was fear, the fear of conspiracy by counter-revolutionaries and/or betrayal by fellow revolutionaries and of assassination, that affected people's thinking. Fearful people may take extreme measures and it is worth remembering the words of Baudot on the Thermidor coup, 'Principles had nothing to do with it; it was a matter of killing'. Or the words of Sieyès who when asked what he had done during the Terror simply said, 'I survived'.

In addition, explanations of people's motives will be affected by the following:

g) our view of them as individuals. If we focus on Danton as the man who tried to end the Terror and as the patriot who rallied the French armies in the face of their enemies, then are we more likely to view him as an idealist?

h) our view of the Revolution as a whole. If we focus on its idealism then we are more likely to believe that the revolutionaries were motivated by idealism rather than the pursuit of power and wealth.

133

Conclusion: Does the French Revolution still matter?

When did the French Revolution end?

I have chosen to end this book in 1802 though that might not be where your course ends and it is certainly not the place where all histories of the French Revolution end.

Simon Schama ends his book, *Citizens* (1989), in 1794 with the fall of Robespierre. To Schama violence was inherent in the French Revolution and this violence found its final expression in the Terror. When the Terror ended so did the Revolution. Now Schama's book is immensely readable, I particularly like the human stories, the citizens whose lives shine so brightly through his narrative. And it is a well written narrative. In his preface he makes the case for **narrative** history, for returning,

narrative
A written or spoken account of connected events

> … to the form of the nineteenth-century chronicles, allowing different issues and interests to shape the flow of the story as they arise, year after year, month after month. I have also, perhaps perversely, deliberately eschewed the conventional 'survey' format by which various aspects of the society of the old regime are canvassed before attempting political description. Placing those imposing chapters on 'the economy', 'the peasantry', 'the nobility', and the like at the front of books automatically, it seems to me, privileges their explanatory force.

But it is important to recognise that Schama is arguing from a perspective that many historians of the French Revolution, and after Chapter 8 I hope this includes you, would dispute. He does have some great one liners, notably, 'The Terror was merely 1789 with a higher body count'. This encapsulates his view. But, like so many politicians' sound bites, for me it oversimplifies a complex situation. First, I would argue that 1789 was illegal popular violence against the State, whilst the Terror was legalised state violence against the People. Second, I would argue that Robespierre was overthrown by a group of terrorists and the continued counter-revolutionary activity after Thermidor showed that the Revolution had not ended. And third, I find the work of Micah Alpaugh (2009) and his claim that the protests of the Revolution were peaceful and only turned violent when they were met with official violence entirely convincing. All these challenge Schama's claims. So I believe 1794 is too early to be seen as the end of the Revolution.

In making my choice I was influenced by William Doyle, author of the authoritative *Oxford History of the French Revolution* (Second edition 2002). In his preface he writes,

> The story still ends in 1802, when Napoleon's power was secure, reflecting my belief that the safest definition of the Revolution is as a series of tumultuous events and uncertainties which only he found the key to terminating. His own tenure of power brought about a new series, but that forms a different (though related) story.

Certainly I would agree that Napoleon's hold on power was not firm in 1799 when he seized it in the Coup de Brumaire. Some argue that as this was a military coup rather than a political change like Thermidor, then 1799 should mark the end of the Revolution. However, it can be argued that Napoleon's position was still open to political challenge. For me it was not until after the Concordat with the Pope and the Treaty of Amiens with the allies were signed, and the plebiscite confirmed him as Consul for life, all in 1802, that Napoleon's position was finally secure. And 1802 to me is a more significant date than 1804 when Napoleon crowned himself emperor. Peter Jones, author of the very popular undergraduate text *The French Revolution 1787–1804* (second edition 2010), would disagree. In his concluding assessment he writes,

> This survey has opted for 1804 on the ground that the substitution of a hereditary empire in the place of an increasingly threadbare republic dispelled any lingering illusions that Napoleon Bonaparte might not be striving for personal dictatorship. Ever since the summer of 1789, voices had been heard declaring that the revolution was now over. By 1804, it really was at an end.

And finally there are some, though admittedly fewer historians, who place the end of the Revolution in 1815. They view Napoleon's rise to power and the changes brought about by his Empire as part of the Revolution. So they see Napoleon's defeat in 1815 and the restoration of the Bourbon monarchy as its end point.

So what do you think, where would you draw an end to the French Revolution?

Reviewing the French Revolution: two activities

1. Reviewing the overview

At the beginning of this book I offered you an overview, the concise French Revolution. By now you will have realised that my version is not the only version possible. Other historians would tell its story differently. For me, during the Revolution France came almost full circle. First, its people deposed their king and proclaimed a republic. They then successfully defended that republic from internal and external attack before succumbing to the rule of an emperor backed by the army. So what is the narrative arc of the French Revolution for you and what eight events make up your concise French Revolution?

2. Assessing the roles of individuals and of the masses

A second way of looking back over the Revolution is to focus on the many individuals who played a part in it. Which of them are the most significant? We can use a number of criteria to answer this question:

- how big an impact an individual had on events during the Revolution
- how big an impact an individual had on peoples' ideas at the time
- how big an impact an individual had on the history of France
- have historians picked them out as significant figures of the French Revolution?

Here are many of the major figures of the revolution:

Marie Antoinette	David	Louis XVI
Barnave	Desmoulins	Marat
Bonaparte	Dumouriez	Robespierre
Brissot	Philippe Égalité	Madam Roland
Carnot	Hébert	Saint Just
Danton	Lafayette	Sieyès

Now as this was the age of the beginnings of balloon flight the idea of a balloon debate may be just the right device to decide which five are most significant figures of the French Revolution. Imagine that all of these individuals, and maybe others that you would add yourself, are in the basket of the Montgolfier brothers' balloon. It is losing height rapidly and only has fuel to carry five people. Any more and it will crash. But to save those five the rest must be thrown out. Using the criteria decide who should be thrown and who should be saved.

Of course, you could choose to differ with this approach. What about the *sans-culottes* and their role in the great *journées*? Do they deserve a place? In fact, do they deserve all five places?

I believe that the biographical approach to the French Revolution has value. For me it is the people in the past that are so fascinating, both the great and the ordinary. And allied to knowing about the individuals I like to have an idea of what they looked like. That is the reason why I find the work of Jacques-Louis David so valuable. In his completed paintings he was never simply trying to depict events as they happened or people as they were. But staged paintings such as *The Tennis Court Oath* or *Marat breathing his last* show us the viewpoint David and other revolutionaries wanted to project and give us an insight into their thinking. Similarly, his sketches of key figures such as Marie Antoinette and Robespierre do more than just convey a likeness; they capture something of the essence of their subject.

The impact of the French Revolution on the people of France

We know what happened to the 'great individuals' but what did the Revolution mean for the rest of the people of France? If we take this at the level of generalisations then:

- the aristocracy may have lost their privileges but most noble families managed to hold on to their lands and, when the Revolution ended, they were able to resume their influence on local affairs
- the clergy also lost their privileges nor did they manage to hold on to their land. Nor did the Church recover its pre-revolutionary level of influence on society
- the bourgeoisie meanwhile were the significant winners in that they had gained land and gained from the fact that careers were now open to people based on talent rather than limited by birth. And when the right to vote was linked to paying taxes it was they who qualified
- the peasantry overall had gained from the abolition of feudalism and some peasants managed to buy land but they were adversely affected by rising rents and conscription into the army
- the *sans-culottes* in the towns who had been so important to the early success of the Revolution were adversely affected by economic events, particularly poor harvests and the decline in value of the *assignat*. And when they lost political power over the bourgeois revolutionary leaders then their demands for a controlled economy were not met
- the poor throughout France suffered the most from the economic difficulties, and the safety net of poor relief from the Church was gone.

Let us leave the last word to Peter McPhee (2006), 'No French adult alive in 1799 was in any doubt that they had lived through a revolutionary upheaval, willingly or resentfully, and that the society in which they lived was fundamentally different.' He points to the French seeing themselves as citizens rather than subjects in a society that became less deferential as the key difference.

Why does the French Revolution matter?

From 1789 right up to the present day and the Arab Spring, whenever there has been a revolution anywhere in the world it has been seen in the context of the French Revolution. The Bolshevik revolutionaries in Russia 1917 saw themselves as modern-day Jacobins and in some ways their struggle mirrored that of the French revolutionaries with civil and foreign war and the emergence of a dictator, Stalin.

The Polish director Andrzej Wajda, in his film *Danton* (1982), used the parallels between revolutionary France and communist Poland, the bread queues, show trials and the language of liberty masking repression, and the parallels between Robespierre and General Jaruzelski, Leader of Poland, to make his contemporary political point. Wajda supported the Solidarity protest movement which was eventually successful in freeing Poland from the one party controlled Communist regime. In one nice small detail he was helped by the fact that both Jaruzelski and Robespierre wore tinted glasses.

▷ Robespierre and Danton arguing, film still from *Danton* (1982), director Andrzej Wajda.

And the events within the French Revolution have resonance for us in Britain. Here, in his comment on one of the episodes of violence that erupted during the peaceful protests in 2010 against the increases in student tuition fees, the cartoonist Martin Rowson draws a parallel between the life of privilege enjoyed by Louis XVI and Marie Antoinette detached from the everyday lives of ordinary people and that of our own monarchy. And he does this with just one word, 'Versailles'.

◁ Cartoon by Martin Rowson, published in *The Guardian*, 11 December 2010.

A writer who sees lessons for modern Britain is Hilary Mantel, twice Booker Prize winner and author of *A Place of Greater Safety* (1992), historical fiction set in the Revolution. In reviewing Ruth Scurr's biography of Robespierre (in the *London Review of Books*, Volume 28 No 8, 20 April 2006) Mantel writes:

> Whatever else he [Robespierre] was, he was a man of conviction and a man of principle. We are not now attuned to principle or conviction, but to the trivia of politics and the politics of trivia. This is why we cannot understand the Islamic world, or the conviction of its militants, their rage for purity, their willingness to die. What they have, the heirs to the liberal tradition have let slip away; we're ironical, comfortable, self-absorbed and fatally smug. We think justice has been done; good enough justice, anyway – and we hope that charity will fill the gaps. Robespierre had no holy book, but he had a militant faith, not in a Christian god, but in a good revolutionary god who had made men equal. He did not see his 'Supreme Being' as a figure who offered consolation alone, but as an active force for change. Revolutionaries were to enjoy an afterlife; death, he said, was 'their safe and precious asylum'. His ferocity of intent, his fierce demand for martyrdom, are suddenly familiar to us; he appears to be our contemporary.

And as this book is published in 2013, in Egypt that revolution is still finding its way. The euphoria following the initial overthrow of the man in power, Hosni Mubarak, has been followed by further violence as those who were once combined in their struggle for freedom now find themselves competing for power. And the old authoritarian system of which he was a part has not gone away. The parallels are there to be seen. So in answer to the question does the French Revolution matter I would answer 'yes', and it will continue to matter as long as people are striving to attain those goals of liberty, equality and fraternity.

Index

Headings in **bold** refer to glossary terms.

Acknowledgements

Photo credits

Cover © INTERFOTO/Alamy; **p.2** © Roger-Viollet / TopFoto; **p.5** © The Art Archive / Alamy; **p.6 & 93** © The Art Gallery Collection / Alamy; **p.7** *t* **& 110** © Gianni Dagli Orti / Corbis; **p.7** *b* **& 114** © The Art Gallery Collection / Alamy; **p.8** © BERTRAND GUAY / AFP / Getty Images; **p.10** © Universal History Archive / Getty Images; **p.11** © The Art Gallery Collection / Alamy; **p.13** *t* © 2003 Topham Picturepoint / TopFoto; **p.13** *b* © INTERFOTO / Alamy; **p.16 & 136** © Gianni Dagli Orti / Corbis; **p.20** © The Art Gallery Collection / Alamy; **p.23 & 37** © The Art Gallery Collection / Alamy; **p.33** © The Art Gallery Collection / Alamy; **p.38** © SuperStock / Alamy; **p.43** © Fine Art Images / SuperStock; **p.44** © Ullsteinbild / TopFoto; **p.45** © INTERFOTO / Alamy; **p.47** © Fabian Bimmer / Alamy; **p.49** © The Art Archive / Alamy; **p.50/1** © The Art Archive / Alamy; **p.59** © James Gillray / The Bridgeman Art Library /Getty Images; **p. 62** © Roger-Viollet / TopFoto; **p.68** © Roger-Viollet / TopFoto; **p.76 & 128** © Musée Carnavalet / Roger-Viollet / TopFoto; p.77 © Roger-Viollet / TopFoto; **p.83 & 131** © The Art Gallery Collection / Alamy; **p.85** © Roger Voillet / TopFoto; **p.94** © The Art Archive / Alamy; **p.102** © The Art Archive / Alamy; **p.103** © Roger-Viollet / TopFoto; **p.104** © Roger-Viollet / TopFoto; **p.106** © The Granger Collection / TopFoto; **p.123** © TopFoto / IMAGNO / Austrian Archives (AA); **p.125** © Musée Carnavalet / Roger-Viollet / TopFoto; **p.127** © INTERFOTO / Alamy; **p.129** © Portrait of a Woman, *c.*1787 (oil on canvas), Labille-Guiard, Adelaide (*c.*1749-1803) / Musee des Beaux-Arts, Quimper, France / The Bridgeman Art Library; **p.138** © 1982 Moviestore Collection / Rex Features; **p.139** © Guardian News & Media Ltd 2010.

Text credits

p.3 'The Execution of Louis XVI, 1793', EyeWitness to History, (www.eyewitnesstohistory.com 1999); **p.9** William Doyle, *The French Revolution: A very short introduction*, (New York, 2001); **p.10** Paul Hanson, *Contesting the French Revolution* (John Wiley & Sons, 2009); **p.10** Peter Jones, *The French Revolution Second Edition* (Longman, 2010); **p.25, 30**, statistics for graphs on **p.53 & 96–97** Colin Jones: extracts from *The Longman Companion to the French Revolution* (Longman, 1990), reproduced by permission of Pearson Education; **p.28** J. Hardman, ed., *The French Revolution Sourcebook* (Bloomsbury Academic, 1999); **p.34** Thomas Kaiser, *French History*, Volume 13, No.3 (2000); **p.36** Andrew Miller, *Pure*, (Sceptre 2011); **p.41** William Doyle, *The Oxford History of the French Revolution*, Second Edition (Oxford University Press, 2002); **p.67** Munro Price, 'Mirabeau and the Court: Some New Evidence', *French Historical Studies*, (Volume 29, No.1, 2006); **p.68** Munro Price, 'Mirabeau and the French Court', *French Historical Studies*, (Volume 29, No. 1, 2009); **p.89** Simon Schama: extracts from *Citizens: A Chronicle of the French Revolution* (Penguin Books, 1989); **p.89** Micah Alpaugh, *French History*, (Volume 23, No. 3 2009); **p.100 & 101** Charles Tilly, *The Vendée* (Harvard University Press, 1964); **p.107, 108 and 124** Ruth Scurr, *Fatal Purity: Robespierre and the French Revolution* (Vintage, 2007); **p.125** Tom Ambrose, *Godfather of the Revolution: The Life of Philippe Egalité*, Duc D'Orleans (Peter Owen, 2008); **p.131** Richard Andrews, 'Social Structures, Political Elites and Ideology in Revolutionary Paris, 1792–94', *Journal of Social History*, Volume 19, No. 1 (1985); **p.132** James Livesey, 'A revolutionary career François de Neufchâteau', *French History*, (Volume 18, No. 2); **p.137** Peter McPhee, *Living the French Revolution, 1789–1799* (Palgrave Macmillan, 2006).

Every effort has been made to trace all copyright holders, but if any have been inadvertently overlooked, the Publishers will be pleased to make the necessary arrangements at the first opportunity.